THE YOUNG PERSON'S HANDBOOK

EDITED BY **ILSE MOGENSEN**

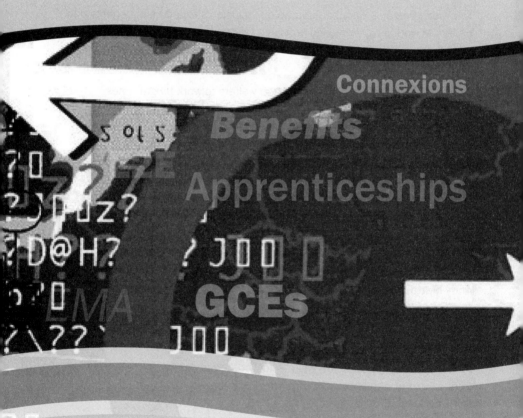

Connexions

Benefits

Apprenticeships

GCEs

THE YOUNG PERSON'S HANDBOOK

About this book

The Young Person's Handbook draws on *Inclusion's* expertise in benefits and welfare to work programmes to provide a reference guide for anyone seeking information on the financial support and provisions currently available to 16-17 year olds.

For information on financial support and welfare to work programmes available to adults of working age, *Inclusion* also publishes the **Welfare to Work Handbook**. For information on our other publications, please visit our website at **www.cesi.org.uk**.

Acknowledgements

We are grateful for the contributions of the following people in producing this handbook:

Neil Bateman for expertise in welfare rights and social policy
Ann Watt for editing the text of the handbook
Robert Spicer for providing the index
Andy Mattock at origin8 creative for work on design and layout.
Jonathan Lloyd for research and advice on young people and homelessness.
Gary Vaux for advice on the benefits section.

Current and former *Inclusion* staff:

Paul Bivand for expertise on welfare to work programmes
Beejal Parmar and **Nicola Smith** for research on education and training
Danielle Mason for researching Chapter 1
Justine Roberts for research and fact-checking
Cait Weston and **Ken Wan** for fact-checking
Becky Shah for proofing and correcting.

Thanks is also due to former *Inclusion* employees **Liz Britton, James Holyfield** and **John Prosser**, who contributed to previous editions of this handbook.

Contents

Contents

1 Overview of financial support

The situation regarding financial support for young people remains complicated; even those who advise young people struggle to understand eligibility and entitlement. There have been some positive steps to simplify the system, and in the long term substantial changes are on the agenda. The Government is keen to associate financial support with learning routes and meaningful activity. Significant increases in the numbers of 16 -19 year olds not in education, employment or training over the last few years have underlined the need for change[1].

In April 2006 a package of reforms was introduced following the recommendations of a 2004 review of financial support for 16-19 year olds[2]. It included:

1. The extension of Child Benefit and Child Tax Credit to families of unwaged trainees on specific Government work-based learning programmes;
2. The replacement of the Minimum Training Allowance with the Education Maintenance Allowance (EMA) for unwaged trainees in England;
3. The extension of Child Benefit, Child Tax Credit and Income Support to cover 19 year olds on courses of non-advanced education or unwaged training started before their 19th birthday;
4. Revised guidance and training for Jobcentre Plus advisers to improve and simplify the processing of claims for JSA by 16 and 17 years olds[3].

Removing the distinctions between education and unwaged training in terms of financial support

The extension of Child Benefit, Child Tax Credit and the Education Maintenance Allowance to cover unwaged trainees is intended to reduce distinctions between classroom- and work-based learning in terms of financial incentives, allowing young people to choose the learning route that best suits them, without having to consider the differing financial implications (see below for eligibility criteria for the EMA).

The LSC has also introduced a contractual requirement for waged apprentices in England to receive a minimum of £80 per week from their employer[4].

Extending financial support to finish education or training courses to 19 year olds.

Because courses of learning up to and including Level 3 take two years, Child Benefit, Child Tax Credit and Income Support for young people over 16 in education or training were previously only available until the young person's 19th birthday. However many young people do not finish their courses by their 19th birthday, often because of disruptions to their education due to illness or leaving care. The new extension of support up to the 20th birthday of young people in education or training should help to ensure that more young people are able to finish their studies.

Revised guidance and training for Jobcentre Plus advisers

Jobseekers Allowance is not generally payable to unemployed 16 and 17 year olds. However, the law allows payment for limited periods. It can also be awarded on a discretionary basis to young people who can satisfy DWP staff that they would suffer severe hardship were they not to receive it [5].

Guidance for DWP staff has been revised to improve and simplify the JSA claim process for young people at risk of severe hardship if they cannot access JSA (with parallel changes for those who claim Income Support while in education and "estranged"). The new guidance states that:

- The young person's own evidence should be believed unless it is 'self-contradictory or inherently improbable';
- If supporting evidence is appropriate, trusted third parties can include Connexions advisers and voluntary and community sector organisations;
- There is no need for confirmation from the young person's parents or carer[6].

Other changes in support for this age group may follow. For example, in March 2007 the then DfES proposed raising the school leaving age to 18[7], and the concept of a universal learning allowance for young people is still on the agenda.

Eligibility Criteria for the Education Maintenance Allowance (EMA)

To be eligible for the EMA you must:

- Be thinking about starting one of the following types of courses in England:
    - a full time further education course at a college or school (such as A Levels, GCSEs or NVQs)
    - an LSC-funded Entry to Employment (e2e) programme
    - a course that leads to an Apprenticeship;
- Be aged 16, 17 or 18;
- Be about to leave, or have already left, compulsory education;
- Have an annual household income of £30,810 or less.

In addition, you will need to have a basic bank account to receive your EMA payments.

If you are eligible, the amount of EMA paid depends on your household income (the combined income of the adults who have responsibility for you in your home). The table below shows how much you will receive for different levels of household income.

Annual Household Income (tax year 2006-2007)	EMA paid per week
up to £20,817	£30
£20,818 - £25,521	£20
£25,522 - £30,810	£10

If eligible, you may also qualify for bonus EMA payments which could be worth up to £500 over a two year programme. You should speak to your school, college or learning provider to find out more about how much your bonus payments could be[8].

Receiving EMA does not affect the value of any benefits that you or your parents or carers may already receive. If you have a part time job while you are on your course, the amount of money you earn will not affect the value of your EMA[9].

For more information you can visit http://www.direct.gov.uk/en/YoungPeople/Money/FinancialHelpForYoungPeople/index.htm or call the EMA helpline on 0808 1016219.

Changes to the machinery of government

Among the new departments set up in June 2007 were the Department for Children, Schools and Families (DCSF) and the Department for Innovation, Universities and Skills (DIUS), which jointly replace the Department for Education and Skills (DfES).

The DCSF is responsible for all aspects of policy affecting children and young people and will lead work across Government on children's health and child poverty. The DIUS has responsibility for further and higher education and skills, aiming to raise participation in post-16 education and learning.

At the time of writing references to DfES links still apply, but the DCSF now has a web link at www.dcsf.gov.uk.

Endnotes

[1] National Statistics, Labour Market Statistics, Labour market status of young people, "Unemployed: Aged 16-17: Not in full-time education: UK" and "Economically Inactive: Aged 16-17: Not in full-time education: UK".

[2] HM Treasury, DWP, DfES, 2005. Supporting young people to achieve: the Government's response to the consultation.

[3] HM Treasury website.

[4] Low Pay Commission Report 2006, National Minimum Wage, Chapter 3.15.

[5] Jobseekers Act, Section 16.

[6] DWP, 2006. "Supporting Young People to Achieve" in Touchbase, March 2006, Edition 42.

[7] DfES, 2007. Raising Expectations: staying in education and training post-16.

[8] See http://www.direct.gov.uk/en/EducationAndLearning/14To19/MoneyToLearn/EMA/DG_066951 "EMA: how much, and how often?"

[9] See http://www.direct.gov.uk/en/EducationAndLearning/14To19/MoneyToLearn/EMA/DG_066945, "What's so good about EMA?"

2 The Connexions Service

If you are considering your learning options to 19 and beyond, whether you are currently in learning or work or not, the Connexions Service should be your first port of call. The Connexions Service will be able to help you to look at your options and even support you while you are in work.

This chapter will tell you what you can expect from your Connexions Service and how to access the Connexions Service.

What is the Connexions Service?

Connexions is a youth support service for all young people aged between 13 and 19. The service aims to provide integrated advice, guidance and personal development with the objective of helping young people to make a smooth transition from education to working life.

You can expect:

- help to review your strengths and weaknesses, understand your situation, recognise your potential and set goals
- advice and guidance on planning to achieve your educational and life goals, including impartial careers advice and guidance
- information and advice where required on health, lifestyle, housing, financial support and other personal issues to assist you in achieving your goals
- information and access to personal development opportunities to broaden horizons and develop talents, including volunteering, community service activities, sports, arts and recreational activities

- personal support and advice and coordinated access to specialist advice and services where needed, to remove barriers to participation in learning and achievement[1]

Connexions is designed to make sure each young person gets what they need and to broker access to specialists who can provide this. The service aims to be coherent and provide continuity in terms of the help you receive. If you require specialist help, perhaps in the form of a housing officer, or social worker, then there will be communication between your Personal Adviser and these specialists. You will not simply be 'passed on' and allowed to 'slip through the net'.[2]

What is a Connexions Partnership?

Connexions Partnerships combines the work of six different Government departments and their agencies and organisations on the ground, together with private and voluntary sector groups and youth and careers services. It is hoped that working and thinking in partnership ensures that Connexions operates seamlessly and is clearly focused on getting results. Connexions Partnership areas consist of several Local Authority boroughs. Local Connexions services have been established at local authority level.

There are 47 Connexions Partnerships in England, set up to mirror the arrangement of Learning and Skills Councils (LSCs).

All Connexions Partnerships should provide young people with:

- an introduction to the service, which explains what services are available and how they can be accessed
- access to information on all education, training, leisure and cultural activities, and all forms of support that teenagers and their parents might need, both locally and nationally.
- access to advice and guidance on the next steps in learning and life. This should include impartial information and guidance on career choices, and more intensive face-to-face guidance from a Personal Adviser for those young people who need it.

- reviews at main transition points – one of these is when you chose post-16 options when compulsory education ends. All young people should have a written record of their next steps.
- personal support where necessary to carry out the next steps
- opportunities to give your views on the service you want and how it should be provided.[3]

Connexions Personal Advisers

Described as 'well-qualified, passionate and enthusiastic practitioners'[4], they are the cornerstone of the Connexions Service.

You may have already come across a Connexions Personal Adviser at school, through social services or perhaps through taking part in activities during the summer holidays (Positive Activities for Young People (PAYP)). Perhaps your school has its own Connexions Personal Adviser or occasionally, especially in year 11, Connexions Personal Advisers came into your school to discuss what you might do when you leave.

Wherever you have come into contact with a Connexions Personal Adviser, they exist to help you to deal with things that you might find difficult in your life and to ensure that you can take up opportunities available to you.

Their role is to get to know you and offer advice and guidance which is appropriate to you. They should keep in close contact with you as necessary and offer you support as you make the choices which affect your future.

Every young person will have access to a Personal Adviser, though not all young people will need a Personal Adviser. Their role is to help you to:

- realise what you can achieve and support you in getting there with advice on routes into employment, training or further education
- build on strengths and tackle weaknesses
- address any personal problems

- explore positive and exciting new ways of developing talents and interests, for example volunteering, community projects, the arts, sport or other leisure activities
- arrange access to specialist support services, if required.[5]

Some people see their Personal Adviser a lot, whilst others might see them a lot for a while, but then stop seeing them when situations change. In some cases, young people mainly contact their Personal Adviser by phone calls or text messages. The amount of contact you have with your Connexions Personal Adviser will depend on your own needs and what is appropriate for you personally.

The Personal Advisers will work in a range of settings, schools, colleges, one-stop shops and voluntary and community organisations.

You do have the freedom to request another Personal Adviser, should you be unhappy with the one you have been allocated. You should have a say in the Personal Adviser appointed to work with you[6].

Personal Advisers will be aware of the boundaries between personal and professional life. That is, while the Personal Adviser will be supportive and caring, they will also maintain professional distance.

The Youth Charter

Every Connexions Partnership should have a Youth Charter which broadly sets out what you can expect from the service, and what you can do if those expectations are not met. A copy of the Charter is available to you from your local Connexions Partnership on request. In many cases, you will probably be given the Charter when you come into contact with Connexions.

The Youth Charter has been designed by young people for young people and is based on the same principles as those that underpin article 12 of the UN Convention on the Rights of the Child.

Two charters should be drawn up. One sets out what you can expect in a general way, e.g. that you can expect to be treated with respect. The other should say more specifically about what is meant by treating you with respect and how the Connexions Service will make this work in reality.

The key elements of the Charter are:

- respect (including equal opportunities and not being judged)
- having a voice and being listened to
- having a choice – encouragement but no pressure
- confidentiality – what will or won't be passed on
- good advice, information and support
- getting help in convenient places at convenient times
- a Personal Adviser who is friendly, honest, well-trained and can be trusted
- a Connexions centre which is friendly and attractive for young people with interesting things to do
- the possibility for young people to get involved in the Service if they want to
- that it is easy to give positive and negative feedback.

While it is the role of Connexions to meet with you at least at key points in your life between 13 and 19, such as when you leave school, for example, you are under no obligation to receive the service. That is, you have a choice – your engagement in the Connexions Service is not compulsory. However, it is extremely likely that it is in your best interests to do so (The Connexions Youth Charter: Guidance for Connexions Partnerships, Appendix 2, 2002).

Connexions can give you information about your other options, should you choose not to use the service.

Connexions at a Glance is a general leaflet explaining what Connexions is. It is available in several languages, in large print, Braille etc. Copies can be ordered from from Connexions Publications,
Tel: 0845 60 222 60 or on the website www.connexions.gov.uk

Confidentiality and informed consent

Confidentiality and child protection issues may arise out of meetings between you and your Personal Adviser. The Children Act (1989) states that in some cases, professionals are obliged to inform other agencies about things that you tell them. This is only the case when there is evidence that you are at risk, or that others are at risk.

You have a right to see what is written in your file and the adviser should agree with you first about entries they make regarding you.

Confidentiality cannot be guaranteed in circumstances:

- where child protection issues are involved
- where there is significant threat to life
- where the young person needs urgent medical treatment
- where potential or actual criminal offences are involved
- where a breach of statutory provision is concerned.'[7]

Informed consent

Personal Advisers may share information about you with other agencies, like social services or Jobcentre Plus. One of the key aims of the Personal Adviser role is to identify those things which might prevent you from participating in learning. In order to do this, it might be necessary to seek detailed information from you and to share this with other agencies you might be in touch with. This is so that any problems you may be facing can be resolved in a more coherent way. For instance, if you have been in care, and are being re-housed, it may be useful for your social worker to know that you are about to start a course at a local college. That way, the social worker can try to re-house you somewhere closer to the college.

In all cases, Personal Advisers should always seek to gain your permission before conferring with other professional workers. Consent should be in writing and it is the responsibility of the Personal Adviser to ensure that you understand: what is being proposed, your right to withdraw consent, and the time period covered by the consent form before asking you to sign it.

When you first come into contact with a Connexions Personal Adviser, depending on the reason for your visit, they will normally ask you to sign a form. This is for Data Protection reasons. If you do not wish the circumstances of your case to be shared with any other agencies or services in any way, you have the right to say so and the right not to sign the form. This does not mean therefore, that you are not entitled to any help or guidance from the Connexions Service.

Connexions staff will inform Jobcentre Plus if you turn down a job or training vacancy, or why you left one.

Connexions and Work-Based Learning for Young People (WBLYP)

Connexions are responsible for placing you in WBLYP (assuming this is what you want to do), for maintaining contact with you whilst you are in training, for helping to address any problems you might have whilst in training, and for helping you with your next step after you have completed training. This might be to employment or to another course of learning.

There are several key elements to Connexions involvement in WBLYP:

- placing you in suitable training
- developing an Individual Development Plan (for those in the Learning Gateway)
- providing regular reviews, particularly for those on Entry to Employment (e2e)
- negotiating with learning providers on your behalf, where problems arise
- finding you another suitable training course, should you leave training for any reason
- helping you fill in form BA1 if you become eligible for Bridging Allowance (see page 67)
- liaising with Jobcentre Plus for benefit applications

However, the Connexions Service is based on individual needs. If you have problems such as trouble at home or concern about relationships, for example, the Connexions Service will provide you with as much support and guidance as is necessary and in a way which is suitable to you.

During training, you will receive regular checks on your progress and your satisfaction with the course.

Towards the end of the course, Connexions staff will give you information and guidance if you need it, on what to do next.

If the Connexions Service helps you into WBLYP, it will make sure that you know about how to keep in touch with the service. Basic information about Connexions will be included in your 'Learning Agreement' which you will get from your training provider.

Connexions and employment

Connexions do have links with employers and will have knowledge about vacancies. However, if you are 16 or 17, and looking for work, it is unlikely that you will be encouraged to take a job without training.

If you are already in a job, you can still use the Connexions Service. They will help you with future opportunities you might wish to take up, which include leisure and recreational activities, advice and guidance on personal development, or any problems you might have, such as housing for example, as well as learning and other employment opportunities.

If you are under 18 and in work, you are entitled to Time Off for Study or Training. Connexions should ensure that you can still access the service whilst you are in work.

Connexions and unemployed/economically inactive young people

Connexions has lead responsibility for 16 and 17 year olds who are unemployed (able to work) or economically inactive (unable to work). Responsibility moves over to Jobcentre Plus for 18 year olds, but this does not preclude further Personal Adviser involvement[8]

Connexions Direct

Connexions Direct is a helpline and online service which endeavours to provide friendly, helpful advice about learning, working, housing, health, drugs, relationships or money. Connexions Direct will call you back if you can't use the phone yourself, for whatever reason. Phone them first or send an email from their website. You can also talk to an adviser online. The service is very quick and easy to access. Advisers are ready to listen to you and can provide information on all kinds of different things.

Advisers are trained and have experience of helping young people. The service is open from 8am to 2am seven days a week. The service is confidential and you do not have to give your name. Calls are recorded to help train staff and to ensure that advisers handle calls properly.

The service is available to young people between 13 and 19. You can find out more by visiting the website www.Connexions-direct.com or by calling 080 800 13219 or texting 07768150850.

Accessing Connexions

You can access Connexions in a number of different ways:-

- At www.Connexions.gov.uk
- Telephone Connexions Direct on 080 800 13219
- Text Connexions on 077 6815 0850
- Drop in centres

To find out where your nearest Connexions Service is, ask at your school, college, or learning provider. You can also find out where Connexions is in your area by using the telephone directory, or asking your Local Authority.

Changes to the Connexions service from 2008

From 2008 funding for Connexions will be transferred to local authorities.

In addition to the advice already given to young people regarding their post-16 options, there will be further targeted youth support for those finding it difficult to make a choice, at risk of disengagement or facing additional barriers to continued participation.

Transition mentors will be provided by Connexions (amongst other places) whereby an adult who has been supporting a young person in school continues to work with them at the start of post-16 learning.

Responsibility for the Client Caseload Information System (CCIS), currently used by Connexions staff to identify what young people are currently doing from 16 onwards (whether studying, working or disengaged) will be transferred to local authorities.

Endnotes

[1] Connexions for All: 2001, Connexions

[2] Connexions at a Glance, 2002, p 5

[3] Connexions Service Planning Guidance 2000, Section G, para 4

[4] Connexions at a Glance, 2002, p 3

[5] Connexions at a Glance, 2002, p 4

[6] Connexions Youth Charter: Guidance for Practitioners, Young People and Connexions Partnerships. 2002

[7] The Connexions framework for Assessment, Planning, Implementation and Review. 2001. para 2.43

[8] The Connexions framework for Assessment, Planning, Implementation and Review. 2001. para 4.6

3 Financial support for those outside learning or work

Under 18 and unemployed

If you are aged under 18 and are unemployed, there are limited circumstances in which you can get Jobseeker's Allowance (JSA).

You or your parent(s) may get short-term payments while you are looking for a suitable training place, in the form of 'extended' Child Tax Credit, Child Benefit or Young Person's Bridging Allowance. The rules for claiming these are explained in this part of the handbook.

The Social Security Act 1988 raised the minimum age for receiving JSA from 16 to 18 years, but some people aged 16 and 17 can still receive JSA in certain circumstances. Others may qualify for Income Support (IS). This is because the Government aims to guarantee a work-based learning place for all young people who are not in work or full-time education between the ages of 16 and 18.

The DWP has powers to make discretionary JSA payments in cases of 'severe hardship'. All young people with little or no money who make a claim for JSA and do not fall into the 'prescribed groups' (see page 32) must be considered for JSA under the severe hardship provisions. The rules for both IS and JSA entitlement are explained in this section of the handbook.

You have a right to make a claim and should not be turned away from your local Jobcentre Plus office. Whether you are considering work, work-based learning or education, or just don't know what to do, you should contact the Connexions Service (or Careers Service if you live in Scotland, Wales or Northern Ireland) which will be able to advise you on your options (see page 12).

The benefits system for 16 and 17 year olds can seem very complex and many of those who advise young people, as well as the young people themselves, are unclear about entitlements. This section sets out the legislation and guidelines in processing claims and giving payments.

Under 16

To be eligible for benefits there is usually a minimum age of 16. This means that any parent or carer whom you live with should claim benefits for you. If you are a parent aged under 16 you can be awarded Child Benefit for your child. However, there is a minimum age of 16 in order to qualify for Child Tax Credit. If you live with your parents or other carers, they may be able to receive Child Tax Credit for your child if they can show that the child normally lives with them or they have main responsibility for the child.[1] They can also receive Child Benefit for you.

Some people under 16 can claim Housing Benefit in their own right – for example, if you have had to take on liability for rent on your accommodation. If you have a disability, your parents or other carers should claim Disability Living Allowance for you but you can receive it in your own right when you turn 16.

If you are entitled, you may receive the following benefits from the day you become 16:

- Income Support
- Incapacity Benefit (and you may count time before you were sixteen as a qualifying period of incapacity for work)
- Carer's Allowance
- Industrial Injuries Disablement Benefit
- Tax Credits

- Guardian's Allowance
- Jobseeker's Allowance (but see the details about who can claim when aged 16 or 17, page 31).

Child Benefit

Child Benefit is a non-means-tested benefit paid to those who are responsible for children under 16, or, up until their 20th birthday if they are in full-time, non-advanced education (up to and including NVQ level 3 and government-funded work-based learning/training, so long as the course/training started before the 19th birthday).

However, there are some circumstances where parent(s)/guardian(s) can claim child benefit for young people older than 16 and younger than 20 who are not in full-time non-advanced education. If you are not living with your parent(s) you may be able to claim Income Support.

Note: Foster parent(s) who have a child placed with them by a local authority do not qualify for Child Benefit for them.

Child Benefit is administered by Her Majesty's Revenue and Customs (HMRC) and claims can be made online at www.hmrc.gov.uk.

Child Benefit Extension Period (CBEP)

If you are 16 or 17, live with your parent(s) and you are not in full-time education or unwaged work-based training, your parent(s)/guardian(s) can claim Child Benefit until the 'terminal date' after you leave school (see page 25) and then possibly for an extended period (the CBEP) beyond that. The CBEP starts the Monday after you leave education/training and lasts for up to 20 weeks. Your parents may also receive Child Tax Credit during the CBEP.

To be eligible for the payments during the CBEP you must be: [2]

- registered as available for work, education or training with your local Connexions/careers service (see page 12)
- not working for 24 or more hours a week

- not be receiving Incapacity Benefit, Income Support or income-based Jobseeker's Allowance
- not in training (Child Benefit and Child Tax Credit would be payable anyway in such a case).

Note: Child benefit can only be paid during the extension period if it was payable before the extension period started.

Date of leaving education or unwaged training	Date child benefit stops ('terminal date')	Date CBEP starts	Date CBEP stops
December – February	Last day in February	First Monday after leaving	20 weeks after start of CBEP
March – May	Last day in May	First Monday after leaving	20 weeks after start of CBEP
June – August	Last day in August	First Monday after leaving	20 weeks after start of CBEP
September - November	Last day in November	First Monday after leaving	20 weeks after start of CBEP

When you can legally leave school

England and Wales

There is only one compulsory school leaving date, which is the last Friday in June.

Scotland

- 31st May if you reach 16 between 1 March and 30 September inclusive
- The first day of the Christmas holiday period if you reach 16 between 1 October and last day of February inclusive.

If you leave school before the legal school leaving date, you will be treated as if you had stayed on until that date.

How to claim extended Child Benefit

Your parent/carer is legally required to make a written request for payment during the CBEP within three months of your ceasing education or training.[3] Before the date you can legally leave school or non-advanced education the Child Benefit Centre should automatically send your parent(s) a letter (form CH298) asking about your future plans. If this does not happen, for example, if you leave school or non-advanced education earlier than intended, your parent(s) can ask about entitlement by calling the Child Benefit Centre helpline 0870 155 55 40 or by writing to the Child Benefit Centre, PO Box 1 DWP, Washington, Newcastle upon Tyne NE88 1AA. You can also notify the Child Benefit Centre online about changes in circumstances via www.hmrc.gov.uk

On the form from the Child Benefit Centre your parent has to give the date on which you registered with the Connexions/Careers Service and has to sign the following declaration:

'I will let you know straight away if s/he starts paid work or a WBLYP course, receives Income Support or Jobseeker's Allowance in her/his own right or starts a course of advanced education.'

Withdrawal of extended Child Benefit

Extended Child Benefit should not be withdrawn if you refuse a job or a WBLYP place during the CBEP. Extended Child Benefit will end when one of the following happens, whichever comes first:

- You apply to receive IS/JSA yourself as a young person.
- You start a job of 24 hours or more a week.
- You start a course of advanced education (e.g. a university degree).
- You reach your 18th birthday (your last child benefit will be paid on the Monday before this date – you may then be able to claim JSA).
- The end of the CBEP.[4]

Reclaiming extended Child Benefit

Child Benefit can be paid again if you leave a job, within the CBEP, whatever the reason for leaving. You will need to register for a job, education or a training place with Connexions/Careers Service. If you have left your job through ill health and you are too sick to go to the office, your parent(s) can contact the local Connexions/Careers Service office, either in person or by phone, to confirm your intention of finding a training place when you are well again.

Your parent(s) can then reclaim Child Benefit, normally on form CH299 available from the Child Benefit Centre.

Child Benefit when a young person is in education or training

While you are under 20 and in 'full-time non-advanced education or unwaged training which is funded by the government,' (known as 'approved training') your parents can claim Child Benefit and Child Tax Credit for you. If you do not live with your parent(s)/guardian(s), and no one is claiming Child Benefit for you, you may be able to claim JSA or IS in your own right (see page 31).

If you are over 16 but under 20 your parents can qualify for child benefit if you:[5]

- attend a full-time course of non-advanced education at a 'recognised educational establishment'
- attend a 'full-time' course of 'non-advanced education' elsewhere, if a DWP decision maker recognises this as education (this may include home tuition if it started before you were 16).[6]
- are on 'approved training'

A 'recognised educational establishment' is a school, college or somewhere comparable.

'Full-time' education is defined as more than 12 hours a week, which includes tuition, exams, practical work and supervised study (in close proximity to a teacher or tutor). Full-time education does not include unsupervised study, private research or meal breaks.

A course of non-advanced education is of a level below a course of advanced education. Advanced education is defined as a course leading to a

- postgraduate degree or comparable qualification or
- first degree or comparable qualification or
- diploma of higher education or
- higher national diploma or
- teaching qualification or
- any other course of a standard above an ordinary national diploma, a national diploma, a national certificate of Edexcel, A levels or Scottish Highers.

'Non-advanced' education, therefore, is broadly defined as all qualifications up to and including A levels, NVQ/SVQ level 3 or Scottish Certificate of Education (Higher level) or Scottish Certificate of Sixth Year Studies.[7] You will be counted as still being in non-advanced education if you are between courses provided that you have enrolled on the course on which you are yet to start or if you are doing unwaged training between courses.[8]

'Approved training' includes:

- in England, 'Entry to Employment' (often known as e2e) or 'Programme Led Pathways'
- in Wales, 'Skillbuild', 'Skillbuild+' and 'Foundation Modern Apprenticeships'
- in Scotland, 'Get Ready for Work', 'Skillseekers' or 'Modern Apprenticeships'
- in Northern Ireland, 'Access' or 'Jobskills Traineeships'

The training must also be funded by the government – for example, through Learning and Skills Councils, the Welsh National Council for Education and Training (ELWa) the Scottish Executive, Scottish Enterprise, Highlands and Islands Enterprise or the Northern Ireland Department for Employment and Learning.[9]

If you are aged 19, you will only be classed as a qualifying young person if you have been accepted or started the course/training before the age of 19,[10] and you will not qualify if you were aged 19 before 10th April 2006.[11]

You are considered as being in full-time non-advanced education or approved training until the 'terminal date' after you leave. A chart showing the four terminal dates is on page 25.

Child Benefit is always paid on a Monday for the period up to the following Sunday. When you leave relevant education, it should be paid up to and including the Sunday following the terminal date, unless you find a job before then.

The Child Benefit paid on this date will cover the period up to the following Sunday. If you become 18 or start work or before this date, Child Benefit stops from the Monday following the day on which you start work or WBLYP, or the Monday of or following your 18th birthday.

If your education or training is interrupted you can have a period of up to six months out of education/learning if it is 'reasonable' (this is not defined in the law) and for longer if the interruption is caused by illness or disability and it is reasonable to ignore the interruption.[12] During a period of interruption, Child Benefit can continue to be paid. It is arguable that this can apply after the terminal date and during the CBEP. Your parent/carer cannot be granted benefit during an interruption period if you start or are likely to start any of the following immediately after the interruption:

- advanced education
- training which is not 'approved training' or
- education linked to employment or an official position in an organisation.[13]

Child Benefit and other benefits

Child benefit is taken into account in full as income for Housing Benefit and Council Tax Benefit, unless the person who receives these benefits is also on Income Support, income-based Jobseeker's Allowance or

Pension Credit. Child Benefit is ignored as income for Income Support and income-based Jobseeker's Allowance if the person claiming also receives Child Tax Credit.

Child Tax Credit

Parents/carers can also receive Child Tax Credit for you while you are in education or approved training in the same circumstances as Child Benefit – there are identical rules.[14] They can also be treated as a parent for Working Tax Credit purposes, which may increase their Working Tax Credit entitlement.

Other benefits

Some parents/carers receive additional amounts of benefits for children and young people. For benefits such as Incapacity Benefit and Widowed Parent's Allowance, if they still receive an increase for a child dependant from before 6th April 2003, this can continue to be paid if you satisfy the Child Benefit rules for participation in education or training. Some people with children, also receive amounts for children and young people in their Income Support or income-based Jobseeker's Allowance because they have not made a claim for Child Tax Credit and the same rules apply to them.

Housing and Council Tax Benefits are calculated using additional amounts for children, whether or not people receive Child Tax Credit. If your parent/carers qualify for Child Benefit because you are in education or training, these additional amounts should be included in the calculation of their Housing and Council Tax Benefits.

When the child benefit extension period ends

At the end of the CBEP, if you have not got a job or training place or if you are not in full-time education, you may apply for discretionary JSA under the severe hardship provisions (see page 46).

Income Support and Jobseeker's Allowance

Some 16 and 17 year olds are entitled to receive benefits. In general, if you are claiming because you are unable to work you should claim Income Support (IS). If you are claiming because you have not yet found work, education or training you should claim Jobseeker's Allowance (JSA).

The age of entitlement for JSA is generally 18. However some 16 and 17 year olds can get it. Though the categories are limited you should never be turned away from making a claim and you should be referred to a 16/17 year-old Specialist Adviser at the Jobcentre. They should contact you within four hours to establish whether or not you may qualify for JSA.[15]

The categories of young people who are entitled are listed below. For each category various additional conditions must be met. The categories and detailed conditions of entitlement are described in turn in the following sections on IS and JSA.

Income Support

Young people entitled to Income Support are:

- Anyone aged 16 or over who is unable to work or to take up training or education (for example, because of caring responsibilities or illness) (see page 34)
- Certain 16-20 year olds who are on a training course (see page 35)
- Certain 16-20 year olds in relevant education (see page 35)

Jobseeker's Allowance for 16 and 17 year olds

16 and 17 year olds:

- may claim JSA during the CBEP (see page 40)
- may claim JSA at any time (see page 41)
- are able to claim JSA under severe hardship provisions (see page 42)

Prescribed groups

Young people entitled to IS or JSA under any of the above categories except the last (severe hardship applicants) are said to be in a 'prescribed group'. (see p. 40-41)

Entitlement to IS or JSA

Single person entitlement

There are two rates of personal allowance for 16-17 year olds: £35.65 and £46.85 per week (2007/08 rates). The higher rate (the same rate as is paid to 18-24 year olds), is paid to a young person who is:

* Eligible for the disability premium, or
* Living away from home for a good reason.

The higher rate can be claimed whenever there is entitlement to IS or JSA, including the severe hardship route, both during and after the CBEP.

Always check whether you are entitled to get the higher rate as mistakes are not uncommon and you may be awarded the lower rate in error, especially if you are getting IS/JSA because you are living away from home.

Couples

If you are married or have a Registered Civil Partnership and you are living with your partner in the same household, you will have to claim as a couple, and will get the couples' rate of benefit (£70.70 if you are both under 18 or £92.80 if one of you is 18 or over).

You will also be treated as a couple if you are living together in the same household as if you were husband and wife (or if a same sex couple as if you were civil partners). You should not be treated as a couple if you spend time together but your partner has a home elsewhere.[16] If you are uncertain whether or not you are a couple or if you have been classed as a couple when you feel that you should not be, it is important to seek independent advice.

If you are a couple who are both unemployed and both of you are under the age of 18, you both must separately establish entitlement to JSA to receive the appropriate couple rate. If only one of you can establish entitlement to JSA then, as a couple, you will receive the appropriate single person's allowance, taking account of the age of the person who claims. If you are a couple where both are under 18, and one of you is ill, disabled or has a child, then your partner should be able to get JSA for you both.

If one of you is aged over 18, then they will be paid the single person's rate unless you also qualify for JSA or Income Support.

Joint claims

Some people have to make a joint claim for JSA. This means that they must both attend interviews and meet the conditions of entitlement (for example to be available for and actively seek work and to make a Jobseeker's Agreement).

A joint claim for JSA is needed if you are a couple who are both aged at least 18 and at least one of you was born after 28th October 1957, unless, for example:

- You have a child/children.
- One of you is in work for at least 16 hours a week.
- One of you meets the basic conditions of entitlement for Income Support (for example, sickness or caring responsibilities).
- One of you is a qualifying young person for Child Benefit purposes.
- One of you is unable to receive income-based Jobseeker's Allowance because of immigration or residence restrictions.

If one of you is aged under 18, you will have to make a joint claim if the person aged under 18:

- Is claiming JSA under the severe hardship rules or
- Qualifies for JSA in other circumstances.[17]

Couples where both are aged under 18 do not need to make a joint couple claim for JSA[18] but to get the couples' rate of benefit, you must both be eligible for JSA.

Income Support (IS)

Entitlement to Income Support

Income Support (IS) is for people who don't have to be available for work. IS can be paid on its own or may be paid as a top-up to other benefits, such as Incapacity Benefit, or earnings from part-time work.

As well as meeting the conditions of entitlement, you will also need to have a low enough level of income and capital to qualify. For more details see Welfare Benefits and Tax Credits Handbook, published by Child Poverty Action Group. Remember that if you receive IS in your own right, your parents/carers will no longer be entitled to benefits for you such as Child Benefit and Child Tax Credit. If you are living with your parents/carers, this may mean that the family income as whole will be less if they are on a low income so it is important to obtain independent advice about your situation before you make a claim for IS.

You are eligible for IS at any time while you are 16 or 17 if you are in any of the following circumstances:

16 and 17 year olds who can't work or do training because you are :[19]

- incapable of work because of an illness or disability (either physical or mental)
- a lone parent
- a single foster parent
- looking after a child under 16 because the child's parent or the person who usually looks after the child is ill or temporarily away
- looking after a member of your family who is temporarily ill
- receiving Carer's Allowance
- regularly caring for someone who has claimed or receives Attendance Allowance or high or middle rate Disability Living Allowance

- a disabled worker
- a disabled student
- registered blind
- expecting a baby in 11 weeks or less, or within seven weeks of having given birth – but not those in relevant education (unless included under another category)
- a 'person from abroad' entitled to benefit in limited circumstances under the urgent cases regulations
- a refugee learning English on a course of more than 15 hours a week – you must have started the course within a year of arrival in Britain and you will be able to get IS for up to nine months.
- a member of a couple looking after a child under 16 while the other partner is temporarily out of the UK
- appealing against a decision that you are not incapable of work
- required to attend court (for example as a witness or defendant).

Certain 16 – 19 year olds in relevant education or on approved training

You can claim IS if you are in relevant education or approved training (see page 27) and you are also in one of the following categories:[20]

- You are a parent responsible for a child who lives in your household
- You qualify for a disability premium in the calculation of your IS entitlement (for example, because you are registered blind or you receive any rate of Disability Living Allowance)
- You are accepted by Jobcentre Plus as being incapable of work for at least 28 weeks
- You are an orphan with no-one acting in place of your parent(s)
- Of necessity you are living away from your parent(s) or any persons acting in place of your parent(s) and they cannot support you because:
    - they are chronically sick or mentally/physically disabled, or
    - in prison, or
    - unable to come to Britain due to immigration laws

- you have refugee status and have started to learn English (on a course or courses totalling more than 15 hours a week) in order to obtain employment, and started during your first year in Britain – you will be able to get IS for up to nine months
- you are a student from abroad who has limited leave to remain in the UK and you are not allowed to have recourse to public funds. If you are temporarily without funds, you may qualify for IS for up to six weeks
- of necessity you are living away from your parent(s) or any persons acting in place of your parent(s) because:
- you are in physical or moral danger, or you are estranged from your parent(s) or any persons acting in their place, or
- there is serious risk to your physical or mental health
- you used to be in the local authority's care and of necessity are living away from your parent(s) or any persons acting in place of your parent(s) (note if you are covered by the provisions affecting care leavers you will not qualify – see page 135). You will not have to show estrangement.

If you are aged 19, to qualify for IS you must also have started or been accepted on your course or training before your 19th birthday.

If you are sick, have left school or full-time education and your parent(s) no longer get Child Benefit for you, you may get IS for as long as you are unable to work or are too ill to go on a training course.

Note: You are treated as being in relevant education until the terminal date (see page 25). So if you leave training, school or full-time education during the summer term, you may be entitled to IS until the last day of August. In September you may be entitled to JSA (see page 41) if you don't fit into one of the other categories of those outside education who qualify for IS.

If you are in local authority care or are covered by the arrangements for care leavers you cannot qualify for IS except in limited circumstances – see page 138.

Definitions of terms

The following guidance is given to the Jobcentre Plus office staff on the use of these terms:

A person acting in the place of your parent(s)

In deciding whether a person is acting in the place of your parent(s), consideration should be given to such factors as whether the person [21]

- provides supervision and financial, social, moral or other care and guidance, and
- provides shelter, food and clothing, and
- is responsible for any necessary disciplinary action

as would be appropriate for a person the same age as the young person.

A person acting in the place of your parent(s) includes:

- Foster parent(s)
- Local authority or voluntary organisation where you are being looked after by them, irrespective of whether or not payment is made [22]

Note: If someone else other than the parent is claiming child benefit or another benefit for you, this is considered a strong indication that this person is acting in place of your parent(s).[23]

In physical or moral danger

This will apply if you would be in physical or moral danger if you lived at home. The danger does not have to come from your parent(s). Evidence from you or your representative that you would be in physical or moral danger should be accepted unless there is 'stronger evidence to the contrary'. But you will not satisfy this unless you are able to show that you have of necessity to live away from home because of it.[24] Legally, there does not have to be a history of harm having occurred for you to be in danger,[25] and it can include situations where you have to live away from parents because of political problems in another country.[26]

Estranged

This is given its dictionary meaning of 'alienated in feeling or affection'.[27] It may be decided that you are estranged from your parent(s) if you have neither the intention nor the wish to live with them and no wish to have any prolonged physical or emotional association with them, or (not and) if they feel similarly towards you. There may be estrangement even where your parent(s) are providing some financial support. However, you will not satisfy this provision just because you say you are estranged. You must also show that you have of necessity to live away from your parent(s) because of the estrangement.[28] According to case law, you can still be estranged even if there is contact as long as there is emotional disharmony.[29] In law, estrangement does not need both you and your parents/carers to not get on with each other – it can be just one of you.[30]

Your evidence about estrangement should normally be accepted and it is only in cases of doubt that additional evidence should be sought. Your parents should not be contacted unless what you say is contradictory or improbable and if a third party (such as a social worker or adviser) can confirm the facts, your parents should still not be contacted. Any contact must only be with your permission and without applying pressure.[31]

Serious risk to physical or mental health

The fact that there may be a risk to your health will not be enough to include you in the category. There must be a serious risk to physical or mental health. This could apply if, for example, you suffer from chronic bronchitis which is aggravated by the damp conditions in your parent(s)' home or if you have a history of mental illness which is aggravated by your parent(s)' attitude towards you. You must also show that because of the serious risk you have of necessity to live away from home,[32] but actual harmful events do not need to have arisen even though the risk must be identified.[33]

How to claim Income Support

Either go to your local Jobcentre Plus office or contact them by phone and say that you wish to claim IS as one of the groups who qualify while in education (do not be put off from making a claim). You can also download the form online from www.dwp.gov.uk/advisers/claimforms/a1.pdf

You should complete, sign and return the form within one month of first contacting the Jobcentre Plus office. This means the claim will be accepted from the date of first contact. To delay may result in a loss of benefit. A Decision Maker decides if you can be paid IS. You will get a letter informing you of the decision. Payment is normally made by payment into a bank or Building Society account (or a Post Office Card Account), though in exceptional circumstances you can be paid by cheque.

As part of the claims process you may be interviewed. You should attend this interview (and if you can't – let the Jobcentre Plus office know so that an alternative interview can be arranged) and it is often helpful to have someone with you at the interview – especially if you are claiming IS while in education under the 'estrangement' or 'risk' grounds.

The standard letter at Appendix 1 may be helpful if you have someone who is helping you with your claim.

If your Income Support claim is refused

If your IS claim is refused, you have a right of appeal to an independent Tribunal. These appeals are often successful, especially if you can obtain help from an independent advice agency.

There are two rates of IS 'personal allowance' for 16–17 year olds, £35.65 and £46.85 per week (2007/08 rates). The higher rate (the same rate as paid to 18-24 year olds), is paid to you if you are:

- eligible for disability premium, or
- living independently (e.g. you are in education and you can't live with parents/carers

Always check whether you are entitled to be paid the higher rate as mistakes are not uncommon and you may be awarded the lower rate in error.

Jobseeker's Allowance

Entitlement to JSA

There are two types of JSA:

- Contributory JSA
- Income-based JSA

Contributory JSA is paid to people who have worked and paid enough National Insurance contributions, so it is very unlikely that 16-17 year olds would qualify. The rest of this section is about income-based JSA.

Claiming during the Child Benefit Extension Period

You may be eligible for JSA if you are in your CBEP and 'of necessity' you are living away from the parental home or the home of any person acting in the place of parent(s) because you:[34]

- are estranged or living away out of necessity, or
- were in custody immediately before the age of 16, or
- were placed away from home as part of a programme or rehabilitation or resettlement under the supervision of a probation officer or social worker, or
- are living away because of physical or sexual abuse, physical or moral danger, or there is a serious risk to your mental health or physical health, or need to live away from home because of a physical or mental handicap or illness, and have needs such as accommodation, or
- cannot receive support from your parent(s) because they are in custody, chronically sick, have a mental or physical disability or are prevented from entering or re-entering the country, or
- have no parent(s) or anyone acting as your parent.

These are similar to those groups who can qualify for IS while in full-time non-advanced education.

If you are married or have a Registered Civil Partnership (or live with a partner as Husband and Wife or as if you are civil partners), you may qualify for JSA, if your partner is:

- 18 or over, or
- 16-17 and registered for WBLYP, or
- a young person who is responsible for a child in the household, or
- a young person who is eligible for JSA/IS, or
- a young person laid off or on short time for up to 13 weeks who is available for employment, or
- a young person temporarily absent from the UK because they are taking their child abroad for treatment, or
- a young person incapable of work and training because of severe mental or physical disability or disease which medical advice says is unlikely to end within 12 months.

Claiming outside the CBEP

There are some circumstances where you will be entitled to eight weeks of JSA. These are if you:[35]

- have been discharged from prison or custody after the child benefit extension period (CBEP) and meet any of the above criteria for claiming JSA during the CBEP
- have stopped living in local authority care and are of necessity living away from your parent(s). However, most young people under 18 who have been in local authority care, cannot receive JSA – see page 138.

Claiming inside and outside the CBEP

You can qualify for income-based JSA at any time if you:[36]

- have been temporarily laid off work or put on short-time – for a maximum of 13 weeks
- are a member of a couple which is responsible for a child who lives in the same household

- would be entitled to claim IS but decide to claim income-based JSA (an adult might do this in order to get NI contribution credits, but there is no obvious advantage for a young person)
- have accepted a firm offer of a job in the armed forces and:
  - were not in employment or training at the time of the offer, and
  - have never had a reduction of income-based JSA because of an employment or training sanction (except for Jobseeker's Direction), and
  - have accepted an enlistment date not more than eight weeks after the offer was made.

Severe Hardship Payments

If you don't fall into any of the above groups and you have little or no money you can still make a claim for JSA. JSA should be paid if severe hardship will result if you don't get benefit.[37]

Technically the payment is made at the discretion of the Secretary of State. In practice, decisions are made on the Secretary of State's behalf either by the Jobcentre Plus office or by the Under 18s Support Team (UEST) in Sheffield. You should be considered for severe hardship payments (see page 46) only if you cannot get JSA in any other way.

How to claim Jobseeker's Allowance (JSA)

Although most young people are not eligible for JSA, the floor-walker or receptionist at Jobcentre Plus should never refuse to let you make a claim.

To claim JSA, including under the severe hardship route, you must be registered for WBLYP with Connexions. However, if you go to the Jobcentre first, they should contact Connexions/Careers service for you.[38] Connexions/Careers will give you a referral form to take to the Jobcentre Plus office, where you will be interviewed. There are a couple of exceptions to this. You do not have to be registered for education, work or training if you:

- are claiming under special rules for people laid off or on short time working
- have enlisted in the armed forces
- have been prevented from registering for WBLYP because of an emergency at Connexions, such as a fire
- would suffer hardship because of the extra time it would take to go to Connexions and register for WBLYP.

If any of the above apply you can register at the Jobcentre Plus office on a temporary basis for up to five working days.[39] The earliest date of contact with either Connexions/Careers or Jobcentre Plus should be treated as the date of claim provided you contact Connexions/Careers or the Jobcentre within five days [40] – this is very important so that you do not miss out on money you are entitled to.

If you do not contact Connexions/Careers after going to the Jobcentre, your claim can be closed down.[41]

You must actively look for education, work and training. There is a three-day waiting period after you claim before you can get JSA, unless you are claiming it under the severe hardship route.

If you have entitlement to Young Person's Bridging Allowance (YPBA) and wish to claim YPBA only, you will have form BA1 from the Connexions/Careers Service. YPBA is not part of JSA. If you wish to claim JSA, you may also be given form BA1, as entitlement to YPBA will be considered before the JSA claim.

If you are in one of the groups which can receive JSA without having to prove severe hardship, you are known as being in a 'prescribed group'.

The Jobseeker's interview

What you need to take to the Jobcentre Plus office:

- Your National Insurance (NI) number, if you have one
- Some evidence of your identity and address
- Your P45 from your last job, if you have one.

If you don't have a NI number, your claim should not be delayed while it is allocated and it is possible for benefits to be paid on an interim basis.[42]

The Jobcentre Plus office should give you the JSA claim forms, JSA1, ES6 and booklet. You should complete these forms before the interview if you have time. You will also be given a form ES9JP or ES11JP to confirm that you have registered with Connexions/Careers. You should also bring these forms with you.[43]

If not, or if you have difficulty completing the forms, you can get help when the forms are checked before your interview starts.[44]

The interview

Interviews should be carried out by advisers who have good interviewing skills and the ability to handle sensitive issues. They must also have a good understanding of:

- the labour market and benefit eligibility conditions for receipt of JSA, particularly
- where the rules differ from those for adults
- the role of the different people and agencies involved with young people.[45]

If you wish, you may have someone such as an adviser, youth worker, relative or friend with you during the interview.[46]

Jobseeker's Agreement

Young people have a special Jobseeker's Agreement, form ES7. The difference from the adult one is in its references to training. It should be drawn up in discussion with you. It will take into account information from your ES9 'Connexions service referral form' and your ES6 'Helping you into work or training'.

The Jobseeker's Agreement lists:

- Your availability for work, including any restrictions
- The type of work and training you are looking for
- The activities you will carry out each week to look for work and training and improve your chances of finding them
- What the Jobcentre Plus office will do to help you
- Brief information on sanctions and disallowances.

You keep a copy of your Jobseeker's Agreement.[47]

Sanctioning

There are various circumstances in which you may be sanctioned while receiving JSA (see page 54). This means that you either receive no JSA or you will receive it at a lower rate. If you are sanctioned, it is very important to obtain independent advice and to submit a written appeal because appeals against sanctions have a high success rate.

If you haven't been sanctioned

If you have never been sanctioned you have certain 'labour market concessions'. You can restrict your availability to training and jobs with suitable training.[48] You can refuse jobs which do not offer suitable training. Non-sanctioned young people are regarded as having good cause for refusing jobs where the training content is not suitable or where no training is offered. A Jobseeker's Direction does not count as a sanction for this purpose.

You must actively seek work and training as a minimum requirement. You can also include steps to find full-time education in your weekly search activities. You must take at least one step each week to find work and one to find training.[49] If it is reasonable in a particular week to take only one step, it can be either to find work or training.[50]

If you have been sanctioned

If you have been sanctioned you lose labour market concessions. That is, you may not restrict your availability to jobs with suitable training, nor can you refuse jobs without suitable training. You must actively seek work. You may not seek training as an alternative to work. However, you may look for training as a step to finding employment.[51]

Jobseeker's Direction

You are given a written statement which tells you what you must do to improve your chance of getting a job. It is given to you to help you find employment, or improve your chances of becoming employed. It will take into account your personal circumstances. You may lose benefit if you cannot show that you had good reason for not carrying out a Jobseeker's Direction.

If you have 'labour market concessions', for example, the right to refuse employment without suitable training, you must not be directed to do something which contradicts the concession. Labour market concessions are not affected by failure to comply with a Jobseeker's Direction. Jobcentre Plus staff are instructed to take care before issuing Jobseeker's directions to people under 18 who have labour market concessions.[52]

The severe hardship rules for JSA Severe Hardship Payments

What is 'severe hardship'?

The law states that: 'If it appears...that severe hardship will result to him unless a Jobseeker's Allowance is paid to him, the Secretary of State may direct that [JSA is paid]' [53].

Severe hardship is not defined in the law and there are no official published rules. However, internal Jobcentre Plus guidance states that 'every claim should be looked at on its own merits and the totality of a person's circumstances considered'.[54] This means that Jobcentre Plus staff must not use blanket rules about what does or does not constitute severe hardship (for example, by stating that you must be living away from home or be homeless in order to qualify).

Some of the personal factors to be taken into account include:

- Your accommodation, and the risk of eviction if JSA isn't paid
- Sources of income and capital
- Health and personal circumstances
- Whether you wouldn't have food or accommodation without JSA.[55]

Note: These are only guidelines and examples. Whatever your circumstances, if you believe you are suffering severe hardship, you should apply for JSA and your case should be looked at. You shouldn't be barred from applying or turned away without having the chance to make a claim. Try to take as much evidence as possible with you to demonstrate the hardship you are suffering, and, be prepared to explain fully why you believe that you are suffering hardship.

All cases are looked at individually and you should mention all the factors which you think are relevant to your case. Payments have been paid to young people who, for example:

- have been unable to find a WBLYP place by the end of their child benefit extension period or by the end of the 40 days' entitlement to YPBA
- are on YPBA but where £15 is not enough to prevent severe hardship – if a severe hardship payment is made in these cases, YPBA will stop being paid
- are living with family or friends who cannot or will not support them financially because, for example, relationships have broken down or they are on benefits themselves or in low paid work.

Jobcentre Plus staff have been known to say that the YPBA is enough to live on and therefore a young person can't get JSA on grounds of severe hardship. That is incorrect if you can show that £15 isn't enough.

How to claim JSA under the severe hardship rules

Looking at severe hardship may form part of a New Jobseeker Interview (NJI). The decision on whether to pay under the severe hardship provisions is made by local Jobcentre Plus staff (or by the under 18s support team – UEST – if the decision is likely to be negative). The Decision Maker must have completed the Severe Hardship Direction training package and hold a Certificate of Authority from the UEST in Sheffield.

If no one with the certificate is present the case can be referred to the UEST. Refusals ('nil decisions') and partner cases must be referred to the UEST in all cases. The certificated officer at the Jobcentre Plus office can decide to pay you JSA under the severe hardship provisions, but they cannot decide to refuse a payment – only the UEST can make a decision to refuse payment.

If you have missed out on JSA, it is possible for a JSA payment on the grounds of severe hardship to be backdated (this should be included in your JSA 5 form) if it is reasonable or you have good cause and your labour market conditions are straightforward.[56] The usual grounds for refusing to backdate is that you have 'survived' without the JSA so you can't have been in severe hardship! The local office can backdate for up to four weeks but if it will be for a longer period, your case must be referred to the UEST.[57]

The certificated officer is responsible for:

- deciding if you would suffer severe hardship if no payment were made
- making directions to pay JSA
- deciding on the length of the direction
- referring relevant cases to UEST
- certain backdating cases .

The following must be referred to UEST:

- Likely refusals ('nil decisions')
- Likely revocations in all cases where a young person has been in the care of the local authority, or where a care order has been discharged

- Couple cases
- If payment is not appropriate from the date of claim
- If backdating is appropriate
- If severe hardship payments have been made for 24 weeks
- All cases where an 'authorised officer' is unavailable
- When permission to contact parent(s)/third parties is refused without good reason
- In alleged abuse cases when a referral to social services is refused without good reason.

The Jobcentre Plus office Decision Maker decides:

- The date of claim
- Whether there is entitlement under a prescribed group
- The rate of JSA payable
- Entitlement reflecting Jobcentre Plus doubts on labour market conditions.

You can appeal against decisions made by Decision Makers. You cannot appeal against discretionary Secretary of State decisions (i.e. that you will not suffer severe hardship), but can ask for a review. In some cases you may be able to take a type of legal action known as judicial review.

The standard letter at Appendix 1 may be helpful if you have someone who is helping you with your claim.

Severe hardship interviews

An interview to gather information about your circumstances will be necessary if you claim JSA under the severe hardship rules.

The Jobcentre Plus officer should record your details on a form known as an ESYP2JP – if you are refused a severe hardship payment, you should ask to be sent a copy.

The interviewer has a list of information that they need to get from you. This includes the items shown below.

The information needed for severe hardship interviews

Information collected at severe hardship interviews
Claim details
Date of claim, name, address, date of birth, NI number, date you left relevant education.
Details of partner, if any.
What you have been doing since leaving school or full-time education or since your last claim for benefit.
Details of last employment and earnings, including what you spent it on if spent.
Are you supported by relatives or friends? Have you ever been in custody?
Other benefit payments (eg DLA) .
Have you ever been in care and are you still the subject of a care order?
Are you living with parent(s) or guardian? If yes, why can't they support you?
If no, why aren't you living with them? When did you leave home?
Can you return home?
Can you return home and be supported financially?
Accommodation details
Type of accommodation and cost.
Do you have access to cooking facilities?
Have you applied for housing benefit?
Will you have to pay any money to the landlord over and above housing benefit?
Is there any risk of eviction if JSA is not paid?
If living with parents/carers, what are their financial circumstances? Do parents receive any benefits for you?
Financial circumstances
Are you getting/have you applied for YPBA?
Do you or your partner have any other income?
Do you have any savings? How much?

Any debts? Type? How much?
Any deductions from benefit payable at present? Any relatives or friends who can help?
Health matters
Are you/your partner pregnant? If yes, expected date of delivery?
Do you or your partner have any health problem?
Miscellaneous
Are you represented by a third party?
If so, type of representative (for example, social worker, friend, relative)?
Why do you think you are in hardship?

Third-party evidence

New rules introduced in November 2005 mean that Jobcentre Plus staff must not normally ask you to get confirmation from your parents/carers that you cannot live with them or be supported by them. The rules say: 'The overriding principle is that the young person's statements should be believed. Only if their statement is self-contradictory or inherently improbable will third-party corroboration be required'.[58]

If it is felt that evidence from a third party is required, Jobcentre Plus staff must ask your permission before making contact and you must sign a statement giving permission.[59] Your permission must be obtained voluntarily and not as a result of threats or inducements[60] nor must you be put under undue pressure to give your permission.[61] Even in the cases where contact is needed with parents/carers, you can refuse permission but it will be important to explain the reasons why.

You can ask a third party (for example, a relative, youth worker, social worker, Connexions/Careers adviser, voluntary organisation worker), to provide additional evidence or confirmation of your circumstances – indeed, such information will help your case.

If you are accompanied at the interview by a third party, the Jobcentre Plus officer should ask them to confirm your evidence.[62] They can also get such information from a responsible third party by telephone or letter. If there is doubt about your evidence or if there is insufficient evidence to satisfy the adviser that you would suffer severe hardship, and it is thus necessary to contact a third party, the Jobcentre Plus officer should consider making you a severe hardship payment for a short period while the evidence is being obtained.[63]

The standard letter at Appendix 1 may be helpful if you have someone who is helping you with your claim.

Allegations of abuse[64]

Jobcentre Plus staff are reminded that this is a very sensitive area. If there are allegations of abuse, a factual written record should be made of:

- the general nature of the abuse
- if the abuse was at home, whether there are any other children or young people living there
- whether their Connexions/Careers Service worker is aware
- whether or not a social worker is helping you.

You will be asked whether or not you are happy for referral to Social Services to take place and the Jobcentre Plus staff member will try and arrange an appointment but they must not put undue pressure on you about this. However, if you refuse a referral or do not attend a meeting with Social Services, Jobcentre Plus will 'consider whether there is still enough evidence to make a direction to pay', but they are warned that 'failure to seek or accept further help does not in itself raise a doubt about the award of a direction'.[65]

Jobcentre Plus may decide themselves to notify the Police and/or Social Services.[66]

Payments of JSA

JSA paid on basis of severe hardship is paid at the higher personal allowance for people under 18 (£46.85 – April 2007-8 rate).

The period for which you will be awarded JSA under the severe hardship provisions depends on your circumstances, but the law does not impose a limit on payments. Jobcentre Plus guidance states that a payment will usually be for 8 weeks.[67] However, a 16-week payment can be made if any of the following will occur in that time:

- You will be 18 within 16 weeks
- If you are pregnant, the 11th week before you are expected to give birth
- You will start a training course, further education or a job.

Payments for shorter periods can be made when:

- A job/training will start
- You will have capital available
- Supporting evidence is not readily available
- You are of no fixed abode.

Stopping (revoking) payments[68]

Your payments can be stopped early (revoked) if:

- Your circumstances have changed so you are no longer at risk of severe hardship.
- You have, without 'good cause', failed to pursue an opportunity of training or rejected an offer of training.
- The original severe hardship direction was based on a mistake of fact, or ignorance of a material fact.
- You return to education (you may then qualify for Education Maintenance Allowance and/or Income Support – see pages 96 and 35).
- You fail to sign on (if you sign on again within five working days and you have a good cause for signing on late, your claim should not be broken).[69]
- You go on holiday (but there are exceptions)

If you stop satisfying basic labour market entitlement conditions – such as attending Connexions and the Jobcentre Plus office as required and being available for and actively seeking work or training – you can cease to be entitled to payments. This decision is made locally by a Decision Maker and so you have a right of appeal.

A revocation is not appropriate where JSA has ceased as a result of a Decision Making Appeal on labour market conditions or where you have signed off.

How to claim again

Severe hardship directions are given for fixed periods only. At the end of these periods JSA ceases automatically and you must re-apply.

The Jobcentre Plus office will re-interview you to review your circumstances. Connexions will be contacted to ask for the same information as at the time of the original claim.

Sanctions and JSA

A sanction means that you either receive no JSA or you will receive it at a lower rate. If you are sanctioned, it is very important to obtain independent advice and to submit a written appeal because appeals against sanctions have a high success rate.

Sanctions and reductions in JSA differ depending on:

- whether you were in work or training before claiming JSA
- whether you receive JSA as a member of a prescribed group or on the grounds of severe hardship
- whether you are a new job seeker
- the action (or lack of action) which led to the sanction.

The rules are complicated and are summarised on pages 65-67.

New job seeker

When you first leave full-time education you are classed as a 'new job seeker'. You stop being a new job seeker if you:[70]

- become employed or self-employed for 16 hours or more a week

- complete a course of training
- give up a training place without good cause
- lose a training place through misconduct .

As a new job seeker, you can turn down one training place voluntarily without good cause without incurring a sanction. This one time is seen as having 'automatic good cause'.[71] 'Turning down' means that you have failed to apply for or accept, refuse, fail to attend, fail to pursue, neglect to avail yourself of or leave a training place.

If you turn down a training place with good cause, then you are still a new job seeker. You maintain your right to one 'training offence' without sanction. This is called 'automatic good cause'.[72]

If you use this automatic good cause and then you commit another training offence, or, where the training place is lost at any time through misconduct, a sanction will be applied. If you have 'actual good cause (see below) you will keep your right to automatic good cause for not having a sanction on a further occasion.[73]

For more information on sanctions, see page 45.

Good cause

Training

If you turn down unwaged training, Job Centre Plus staff must consider any potential 'good cause'. This phrase is not defined in the law, but here are some of the things which Jobcentre Plus staff should use to decide whether or not you have good cause. This list is not exhaustive and does not carry legal force, so even if your circumstances are not covered by the following, you may still be able to argue that you have good cause:[74]

- Disease or physical or mental disablement which affected your ability to attend training or put your or others' health at risk. (The Jobcentre Plus Decision Maker should first consider whether this means you are incapable of work, but you do not need to be incapable of work in order to have good cause.)[75]
- A sincerely held religious or conscientious objection.

- Travelling time to and from training is more than an hour either way. (Particular circumstances have implications here, for example, if there is no learning provider within one hour of where you live).
- Attendance at court as a witness or party to proceedings
- Caring responsibilities – where no other household member or close relative of the person being cared for was available to care for the person and it was not practical for you to make alternative care arrangements.
- Arranging or attending a funeral if the deceased is a close relative or friend.
- You had to deal with a domestic emergency. The nature of the emergency will be considered, and your availability for/actively seeking work status may be questioned
- You are undertaking emergency duties – performing the duties for the benefit of others in an emergency.
- Health and safety at risk by participating.
- The training was unsuitable,[76] but you will usually be expected to have tried to use the complaints procedure before leaving. Decision Makers are reminded that your age and lack of experience may mean that you are not familiar with or too frightened to use such procedures and so you may still have good cause if you did not make a complaint.[77] You will have good cause if a Connexions/Careers adviser informed you that the training was unsuitable and that you should leave/not attend/apply.[78]
- Attendance or participation would mean that you would breach a Community Order or Disposal or Anti-Social Behaviour Order.[79]
- Disruption to part-time study.[80]

Employment

Reference in the DWP guidance about 'good cause' to neglect a reasonable opportunity of a place on a training course is the same as that used for 'neglecting a reasonable employment opportunity'.[81]

Not a new job seeker

If you are not a new job seeker the following sanctions and reductions apply.

A Jobcentre Plus Decision Maker imposes a sanction on a claimant, if the claimant is entitled to JSA and has :[82]

- lost employment through misconduct
- left employment voluntarily without just cause
- refused or failed to apply for or accept employment without good cause
- neglected a reasonable opportunity of employment without good cause
- refused or failed to carry out any reasonable job seeker's direction
- lost a place on a training scheme or employment programme through misconduct
- given up a place on a training scheme or employment programme without good cause
- failed to attend a training scheme or employment programme without good cause
- refused or failed to apply for or accept a place on a training scheme or employment programme without good cause
- neglected a reasonable opportunity of a place on a training scheme or employment programme without good cause.

Leaving employment

If you leave employment (including employed-status Modern Apprenticeships) voluntarily 'without just cause' or because of your misconduct you are sanctioned in the same way as an adult, and the case is referred to the Decision Maker in the same way as an adult case. JSA is not suspended while waiting for the decision but your JSA can be stopped for between one and 26 weeks if the Decision Maker decides against you.

There is a lot of case law on this which can help you successfully challenge a sanction imposed on employment grounds. The length of the sanction can be appealed too – it is common for the full 26 week sanction to be imposed when a shorter period would be more appropriate. When deciding the length of a sanction, the Decision Maker must consider:

- if a job was due to last more than 26 weeks, how long it would last
- if you are to be re-engaged by the same employer, the date you will be re-engaged
- if the job was for less than 16 hours a week, the rate of pay and hours of work in the job
- any mitigating circumstances of physical or mental stress connected with the job.

Case law dictates that the discretion about length of sanctions must be exercised judicially, taking account of all the circumstances and justice and merits of your case.[83]

You can apply for payments under the JSA hardship provision in certain circumstances (see page 63). Don't confuse JSA paid on the grounds of hardship (when you are sanctioned) with JSA paid on the grounds of severe hardship when you are 16/17.

If you were unemployed for 13 weeks and then took a job, working at least 16 hours per week, there is a 'trial period' from the fifth to the twelfth week when you can leave for any reason other than misconduct, without incurring sanctions.[84] This is called Employment on Trial.

If you leave training (non-employed status) voluntarily without good cause and claim JSA as a member of a prescribed group (see page 32) or on the grounds of severe hardship, you will be sanctioned by having your JSA reduced for a set period of two weeks. It will be reduced to 60 per cent of the normal amount, or to 80 per cent if you or a member of any family you claim for is seriously ill or pregnant.

Refusing to take up employment

If you refuse or neglect to avail yourself of employment (including employed-status training) you can be sanctioned unless you still have your 'labour market concession'. This is a right to refuse jobs which do not offer 'suitable' training, which you usually have if you have not previously been sanctioned (see page 45). Your JSA will be reduced for two weeks, or until your 18th birthday if that is sooner.

The Jobcentre Plus office or Connexions must have offered you the job. If you refuse training (not employed-status) and you are claiming JSA as a member of a prescribed group your JSA can be reduced to 60 or 80 per cent for two weeks.

If you refuse training and you are claiming JSA on grounds of severe hardship, your payments can be revoked (stopped). If you make a new claim, your payments will be reduced to 60 or 80 per cent for the first two weeks.

Internal guidance asks Connexions/Careers staff to tell Jobcentre Plus promptly if they think you have refused employment/training or have neglected to avail yourself of a suitable opportunity of employment/ training using forms ES22 or ES95N.[85] This guidance appears to undermine the role of Connexions staff as advocates for young people and may be open to legal challenge.

You should ask to see any such information and seek independent advice.

Prescribed group

For prescribed groups, cases of refusal or premature termination of training or leaving because of misconduct are decided by the DWP Decision Maker. If you leave a place, you will be given a form ES86Y by the Jobcentre so that you can state the reasons why you left. If misconduct is involved, the learning provider will be asked for information.

Severe hardship claimants

If you are claiming JSA on grounds of severe hardship, such cases are not determined by a Decision Maker. The Jobcentre Plus office adviser, on behalf of the Secretary of State, decides whether you had good cause.[86] If you had good cause to leave training, a certificate of good cause will be issued.

If you refuse a place, the Connexions/Careers Service notifies the Jobcentre Plus office which checks its evidence against evidence from you that you think establishes good cause. If more evidence is required, you should be invited to explain your refusal at an interview at the Jobcentre Plus office as soon as possible. If you do not attend, it will be assumed you don't wish to comment.

If the Jobcentre Plus adviser doesn't consider there was good cause, payment is automatically reduced for the first two weeks of your new claim for JSA.

If you fail to complete a training course, the Jobcentre Plus office adviser will decide if you had good cause, after considering evidence from Connexions and from you. If they decide that there is good cause, a good cause certificate will be issued and a copy given to you. A good cause certificate will be issued whether the good cause was actual or 'automatic', that is, you were a new job seeker with a right to one 'training offence' (see page 56 for more information about leaving a training course which you believe to be substandard).

If the Jobcentre Plus office adviser decides that there was not good cause, or if there was misconduct, you will get a Decision Certificate ES91 and your payments will be reduced to 60 or 80 per cent for two weeks.

Misconduct

It is up to the person who alleges that you committed misconduct which resulted in your losing your job or training place to prove it – usually the learning provider. For Jobcentre Plus office staff to decide you committed misconduct, it must be more likely than not that the allegations are true. You will be given a chance to comment on statements made against you by the provider or witnesses, before a decision is made – it is important to do so and if you don't reply within a week, Jobcentre Plus staff are advised to consider a sanction.[87] (There is no basis in law for Jobcentre Plus staff to impose a one week deadline and this procedure may be unlawful).

What is misconduct?

Misconduct is not defined in regulations, but case law describes it as being blameworthy and wrong conduct, connected directly or indirectly to your activities on the training course or job.[88] Simply being inefficient or breaking minor rules or doing something which you did not know was wrong will not usually amount to misconduct, even if it gives grounds for your employer/training provider to dismiss you.[89] Misconduct can also happen outside work, for example, being convicted of an offence of theft outside work which means that your employer cannot let you work with valuables.[90]

The following may be considered as misconduct:

- Wilfully disobeying a reasonable order (unless you had a good reason)
- Actions outside the training place which affect your suitability for the training: failure to follow regulations (for example, rules of safety)
- Refusing to do appropriate work
- Refusing to work overtime – this only counts if it is explicitly set out in your learning agreement and adequate notice was given
- Negligent or inefficient work – a lot of factors are taken into account before a decision is upheld on this, including the seriousness of the omission, the extent to which you are to blame and the level of skill and responsibility expected of you
- Offensive behaviour, quarrelling and fighting
- Dishonesty

The following are not misconduct:

- Refusal to do work that is not part of the learning agreement
- Refusing to work overtime if it is not explicitly mentioned in the learning agreement, or if the request is not reasonable or adequate notice is not given
- Inefficiency if you were doing your best – inefficiency can be misconduct only if you are failing to meet standards within your capabilities
- Being a naturally slow worker

- Cases in which there is medical evidence that you were not responsible for your actions due to mental illness
- Cases in which you have been dismissed for absence but have obeyed all the rules regarding notification
- Failure to obey an instruction because of a misunderstanding
- Refusal to perform tasks because of a genuine religious or conscientious belief
- Work as a self-employed person which has been terminated.

Misconduct is not the same as reasonable cause for dismissal. In some circumstances, it might be reasonable to dismiss you for inefficiency, for example, but inefficiency is not usually misconduct and your benefit should not be sanctioned.

What is leaving employment voluntarily without just cause?

You should only be classed as leaving voluntarily if you have done so of your own free will and without any coercion and if it is something you have brought upon yourself.[91] If you volunteer for redundancy when your employer is planning to cease trading or wishes to lose jobs,[92] this will also not be leaving voluntarily nor will you be if your employer changes your terms and conditions of employment without agreement[93] provided that you tried to change matters. You must show that what you did was reasonable and that generally you took steps to resolve problems and look for alternative work before claiming JSA.

You may have just cause for leaving voluntarily if:[94]

- you were not aware of the terms and conditions of a job when you agreed to take the job
- you have pressing or urgent domestic or personal circumstances
- you have a genuine grievance about the job but have been unable to resolve it
- you were not suited to the type of work and thought it better to leave rather than be dismissed
- you were asked to do work outside your normal or contractual duties

- the work conflicted with sincerely held religious or conscientious beliefs
- you left because you obtained a better job and it fell through
- you left to take up study or training
- the job was affecting your health or safety or it was beyond your capacity
- you were having to live away from home for long periods.

These are just examples.

JSA hardship provision

This is not the same as severe hardship provision. It is JSA paid at a reduced rate in certain circumstances to people in hardship. You can apply for payments under the JSA hardship provision if your JSA has been stopped or you are waiting for a decision.

In all the situations below, if you are claiming JSA as a member of a prescribed group (see page 32), you must show that you or a member of your family would suffer hardship if hardship payments were not made.

If you are claiming JSA on grounds of severe hardship and are waiting for a decision or have received a benefit penalty, you are entitled to hardship payments. You do not have to prove you will suffer hardship as you have already proved severe hardship. But you cannot get hardship payments if you have failed to fulfil labour market conditions.

You can apply for hardship payments in the following circumstances:[95]

a) JSA has been refused because you do not satisfy labour market conditions

You can claim hardship payments if JSA was refused because you are not available for work, not actively seeking employment and training, or will not complete and sign a satisfactory Jobseeker's Agreement.

If you are claiming JSA on grounds of severe hardship, you cannot get hardship payments when you do not satisfy labour market conditions.

b) You have been sanctioned

Most sanctions are for two weeks and include automatic entitlement to a reduced rate of JSA without the need to apply for hardship payments. But for some employment offences, JSA is stopped (not reduced) for a period of one to 26 weeks. You get no payment unless you successfully claim hardship.

c) You are waiting for a decision on whether you satisfy certain labour market conditions at the start of a claim and your JSA claim has not been processed

These conditions are whether you are available for work, actively seeking employment and training, and have completed and signed a Jobseeker's Agreement.

d) Your JSA has been suspended until a decision is made on whether you satisfy certain labour market conditions

Note: These are the same conditions as in (c).

The amount of hardship provision is your normal amount of JSA reduced to 60 per cent, or reduced to 80 per cent if you or a member of your family are pregnant or seriously ill.

If you are getting hardship payments you do not get credits of National Insurance contributions. However, if you are paying rent, you will still be entitled to Housing Benefit even if you have had your JSA stopped or paid at a reduced rate.

How to claim

You will have to attend an interview at the Jobcentre Plus office and fill in an application form.

Jobcentre Plus staff should not discourage you from applying for hardship payments.

Awards of JSA hardship payments are usually paid two weeks in arrears. You can apply for a Social Fund crisis loan payment to cover the time before the first payment is due (see page 81), but the loan will be repaid by deductions from your benefit.

You will have to attend the Jobcentre Plus office for interview every two weeks before you get your payments.

Special rules apply about claiming if you use the postal facility. In this case, the relevant claim form must be requested, completed and returned to the Jobcentre Plus office. You must supply your contact details in case of any queries. A decision will then be made about whether you satisfy the hardship criteria without you attending an interview.

3

Summary of JSA sanctions

The rules about sanctions are extremely complicated. We summarise the main rules here. Look up the reason for a sanction in the table below, then check what the relevant sanction is.

Prescribed group/non-severe hardship group

Sanction Type	Period of Sanctions (weeks)	Decision Method	Effect on Payment
Misconduct (employment)	1 -26	SDM	Hardship – by application, not automatic
Misconduct (training)	2	SDM	Automatic reduced rate of JSA
Leaving training early	2	SDM	Automatic reduced rate of JSA
Neglect to avail	2 *	SDM	Automatic reduced rate of JSA
Refusal of training	2	SDM	Automatic reduced rate of JSA
Jobseeker's Direction	2	SDM	Hardship – by application, not automatic

Severe hardship group

Sanction Type	Period of Sanctions (weeks)	Decision Method	Effect on Payment
Misconduct (employment)	1-26	SDM	Hardship – by application, not automatic
Failure to complete training (Including misconduct)	2 (imposed from start of next direction)	Adviser	Automatic reduced rate of JSA
Rejecting an offer/ failure to pursue an opportunity of training	2 (imposed from start of next direction)	Adviser	Automatic reduced rate of JSA
Neglect to avail	2 *	SDM	Automatic reduced rate of JSA
Jobseeker's Direction	2	SDM	Hardship – by application, not automatic

Note *: Sector Decision Makers may give 1–26 week sanctions; however the reduction is only applied for the maximum of two weeks.

Reductions in benefit incurred through the sanctions regime amount to either 40 per cent or 20 per cent reductions. You will normally have your benefit reduced by 40 per cent unless you or a member or your family is pregnant or seriously ill.

Behavioural problems

Guidance issued to Connexions advisers states that 'a young person on JSA who is finding it difficult to seek or has had difficulty sustaining training or work because of challenging behaviour may have an underlying medical condition (physical or mental) which may make them incapable of work for state benefits purposes'.[96] Connexions/Careers Service staff are advised to notify Jobcentre Plus about this and to help the young person to make a claim for Incapacity Benefit.

Young Person's Bridging Allowance (YBPA)

In this section, the term WBLYP means Modern Apprenticeships (MA) at either Foundation or Advanced Level and other training (including e2e).

Young Person's Bridging Allowance (YPBA) is not part of the social security system and does not have detailed legal rules. Instead it is based on internal Jobcentre Plus guidance found in Chapter 4 of the Jobcentre Plus Allowance Payments Guide. You can obtain a copy of this document from your local Jobcentre Plus office by making a request in writing and saying that you are requesting it under the Freedom of Information Act 2000. General legal principles of fairness and hearing your version of events still apply to how Jobcentre Plus administers YPBA.

YPBA is a payment made by the Jobcentre Plus office. It is worth £15 a week, calculated at £3 a day from Monday to Friday. It can be paid for up to eight weeks in a 52 week period (but if you have a disability, there is no time limit). Young Person's Bridging Allowance (YPBA) is a financial concession to help you to pay for any additional expense you may incur in seeking a training place. It is not intended to be a payment to live on. If you would experience severe hardship trying to live on YPBA alone, you should consider making a claim for Jobseeker's Allowance under the severe hardship rules instead (see page 46).

You are eligible for Young Person's Bridging Allowance (YPBA) if:

- you are under 18
- you have left a job or training place, even if you were in work/training for just one day after the end of the CBEP (or immediately after the CBEP if you are disabled)

- it is after the CBEP

- you are not in full-time education (including an Entry to Employment course)

- you are not in paid employment for more than eight hours a week between Monday and Friday.[97] You must also sign a statement agreeing to give up such work if a suitable training place becomes available.[98]

You must also be:[99]

- willing and able to take up a suitable training place, and

- registered with Connexions/Careers Service for WBLYP. YPBA can be paid immediately following the end of the CBEP to:

- a young person who has a health problem or disability

- a young person who has been sick during the CBEP

- a former detainee who has been in custody during the CBEP

If you refuse a suitable training place without good cause, you can be refused a YPBA on the grounds that you are voluntarily unemployed.

If you have left a job it must have been paid employment (including self-employment and casual/temporary employment or work abroad), undertaken between Monday and Friday, for more than eight hours a week.[100] Just one day of work is sufficient.

YPBA is payable from the date of registration for WBLYP with Connexions/Careers service. It is paid for a maximum of eight weeks (calculated as 40 weekdays) in a period of 52 weeks, unless it is accepted that you have a disability or health problem, when there is no limit until the age of 18.

If you have used up all of your eight weeks' entitlement to YPBA, you will have to wait a full 52 weeks before becoming entitled again and you must have also left a job or WBLYP. The 52 week period starts from the first day of payment. It is payable fortnightly in arrears.[101]

The Jobcentre Plus office will notify the Connexions/Careers Service if you are successful in your claim for YPBA and Connexions will notify the Jobcentre Plus office if you take up, or refuse without good cause, a

WBLYP place. You can have left your job or WBLYP for whatever reason and still be entitled to YPBA. But YPBA may be withdrawn if you refuse to accept a further offer of a WBLYP place. Connexions/Careers Service will notify Jobcentre Plus if they feel that you have refused a suitable training place without good cause – you should ask Connexions to provide you with a copy of any evidence and communications about you and it may be possible to take legal action against Connexions/Careers Service if they have not acted fairly or if the evidence is incorrect.

The Child Benefit Extension Period and YPBA

YPBA is only payable outside the CBEP whether or not Child Benefit has been paid. So, if you lose, or leave, your training place during the last eight weeks of the CBEP, Child Benefit will normally be paid for the rest of the extension period. A balance of YPBA can be claimed at the end of the CBEP.[102]

If a claim is made within one calendar week of the CBEP, YPBA would be payable from the first day after the end of the CBEP.

If you lose or leave a WBLYP place in the final week of the CBEP, it is not necessary for your parent(s) to apply to the Child Benefit Centre to reinstate the Child Benefit. You will be paid YPBA from the first day after the end of the child benefit extension period, provided you register with Connexions/Careers Service for a WBLYP place within one calendar week of the CBEP.[103]

Child Tax Credit extension period and YPBA

YPBA is not payable during the 20 week extension period if Child Tax Credit is being paid for the young person. However, if the young person starts and then loses a WBLYP or job in the 20 week period, unlike Child Benefit, Child Tax Credit is not re-instated. Therefore, in these circumstances, a young person may be entitled to YPBA, providing normal eligibility rules are satisfied.

Note: Even though the 20 week extension period may be current, Child Tax Credit may not actually be in payment. If this is the case, YPBA can be paid.[104]

Young people from abroad

Foreign nationals

If you are a citizen of a country outside the UK, whose parent(s) are not eligible for Child Benefit during the CBEP, you are not entitled to YPBA when you first arrive in this country. However, if your parents do receive Child Benefit or if you are eligible for WBLYP and you subsequently get a job, or WBLYP, and then you leave it, you can be paid YPBA.[105]

UK nationals

YPBA may be paid if you are a UK national returning to the UK and if:

- you return after the CBEP
- you lived with your parent(s) while abroad
- your parent(s) were entitled to child benefit during the Child Benefit Extension Period
- you apply for YPBA after the Child Benefit Extension Period
- Child Tax Credit extension is not in payment, and
- you have registered for WBLYP with Connexions/Careers Service.[106]

In this case there is no requirement for you to have lost or left a WBLYP place to qualify.[107] If you have been abroad to work, and return after losing or leaving a job, you will be eligible to receive YPBA for the 40 day period, provided that you meet all the other eligibility criteria.

Disability and YPBA

YPBA can be paid immediately after the end of the Child Benefit Extension Period if you are disabled, even if you have not been in work or training.[108] You still need to register for WBLYP if you have a health problem or a disability. If you receive Disability Living Allowance, this has no effect on your entitlement to YPBA.[109]

If you have a disability, you are eligible for YPBA for the length of time it takes you to find a suitable WBLYP place or a job, or, until the day before your 18th birthday, not just for 40 days.[110]

The definition used to decide whether or not you have a disability is very broad (you don't need to be receiving any benefits for your disability) and it is the same definition used in the Disability Discrimination Act 1995,[111] which defines a disabled person as someone who has: 'A physical or mental impairment which has a substantial and long-term adverse effect on their ability to carry out normal day-to-day activities.'

You will need to fill out form BA1: 'Application for Young Person's Bridging Allowance' and then form BA8: 'Young Person's Bridging Allowance – Health Problems and Disabilities'. The Jobcentre Plus office checks it and can then endorse your status. If there is a dispute about whether you are disabled, only a court or tribunal can decide this point. If you have difficulty in attending the Jobcentre Plus office, you may apply by post.[112]

Note: Although YPBA can be paid after the end of the extended Child Benefit in these cases it cannot be paid if Child Tax Credit is in payment.

Ex-offenders and YPBA

If you are discharged from custody during the CBEP, Child Benefit may be restored. If you were in custody on the CBEP cut-off date, YPBA is payable for the normal 40-day period without the need to have left a job or a WBLYP place.[113] If you have left custody and have to live independently of your parent(s), you are entitled to JSA for the first eight weeks after you have been discharged as a 'prescribed group'. If you have not found a suitable WBLYP place by the end of the eight weeks, then you should be advised by the Jobcentre Plus office to make a claim for JSA on severe hardship grounds.[114]

Jobseeker's Allowance and YPBA

In some cases a young person may claim JSA and subsequently not satisfy the conditions but have an underlying entitlement to YPBA.[115] For instance, as a young person who is outside full-time education and work, and therefore guaranteed a training place, it is possible to have an underlying entitlement to YPBA. At the same time you can be entitled to JSA if you are in one of the 'prescribed groups'. Ex-offenders having to live away from parents are an example. So while you might be entitled to both you would never be paid both. Whether the YPBA is regarded as income, or 'ceases to be paid', the net amount remains the same. An entitlement to JSA does not exclude you from an entitlement to WBLYP.

Housing Benefit and YPBA

If you are living away from your family and have responsibility for paying rent you may be eligible for housing benefit while you are on YPBA. You should claim this from your local authority. You should also make a claim for JSA (see page 42). You do not need to be receiving YPBA to qualify for Housing Benefit.

National Insurance (NI) and YPBA

Class 1 credits of NI contributions are not awarded to under-18s on YPBA. People under 18 are automatically awarded Class 3 credits up to and including the year of their 18th birthday.

How to claim YPBA

To claim YPBA you should register with the Connexions/Careers Service and pick up the form BA1. You need to complete sections A, B and C; the Connexions/Careers Service should fill in section D. The Connexions/Careers Service should phone and make an appointment for you at the Jobcentre Plus office.[116] Take the completed BA1 to the Jobcentre Plus office, where your claim will be processed.

If you attend the Jobcentre Plus office without the form, the receptionist should make an appointment for you with Connexions/Careers Service so you can register for WBLYP. At the same time they will make an appointment for you to see a Young Person's Bridging Allowance officer, so that you may return with the completed form and begin to process your claim.[117]

If you have been to Connexions and have a completed form and then fail to go to the Jobcentre Plus office to make the claim, they will notify Connexions of your non-attendance.

You will have to attend the Jobcentre regularly ('sign-on'), normally every two weeks, in order to continue to receive YPBA .

Backdated claims

If you attend the Jobcentre Plus office more than two days after you registered for WBLYP with Connexions/Careers Service, you will be asked for an explanation. If you have a good reason (for example, if you were looking for work or training or there was an illness in the family), then you should be paid from the date of initial registration.[118] If it is felt that you do not have a good reason then the allowance will be paid only from the date of the claim at the Jobcentre Plus office rather than from the initial registration with the Connexions/Careers Service. However, this may be open to challenge because there is no legal basis to this rule. Either way, you will still be entitled to 40 days of YPBA (or longer if you have a disability – see page 122)

If you qualify for YPBA you must attend the Jobcentre Plus office fortnightly to sign a declaration. YPBA is paid fortnightly in arrears by Automatic Credit Transfer to a bank account. In certain circumstances young people with disabilities or living in areas with poor transport facilities can claim YPBA by post.

Similar rules apply for late attendance. If your fortnightly application is not made on the allocated 'signing day', Connexions/Careers Service will be notified and will contact you to remind you to attend. If you do not attend within five working days your claim will be terminated.

Community Service Orders

If you are subject to a Community Service Order from the courts or attend a day centre as part of a sentence from the court, the Jobcentre Plus office should try to fit in your attendance with your community service attendance hours. If you are available to take up training YPBA will be paid.[119]

Eligibility for YPBA

To be eligible for YPBA, you must apply for a WBLYP place, make yourself available for interviews when required and be prepared to start on a WBLYP course at any time.

Holidays

If you go on holiday and state that you are not available to accept a WBLYP place during the holiday period, YPBA should not be paid for any days that you say that you will be or have been on holiday. You can get YPBA if:

- you are not going abroad, and
- you offer to be available for WBLYP while on holiday, and
- you sign a statement with
    - dates of the holiday
    - an address or telephone number where you can be contacted
    - a declaration that you are willing to return for a WBLYP place or interview .[120]

When you return from holiday, when you next sign on, Jobcentre Plus will ask you to confirm the dates that you were away.

Holidays abroad

YPBA is not payable for any day that you are outside Great Britain, Northern Ireland or the Isle of Man.[121]

Sickness

If you are sick and unable to work or do WBLYP, you will no longer be eligible for YPBA and should be referred to the benefit section of the Jobcentre Plus office to claim Incapacity Benefit or Income Support. If you notify Jobcentre Plus that you are unable to take up training because of sickness, YPBA will be paid up to the last date that you were fit to take up training.[122] When your sickness ends, you will need to register again with Connexions/Careers Service and obtain a new BA1 to re-claim YPBA.[123]

Part-time education

You can receive YPBA if you attend college for less than 16 hours a week providing you:

- satisfy the normal eligibility rules for YPBA, and
- sign a written statement on an ES589 that you are willing to give up your studies to take up a training opportunity, and
- are available to attend interviews on the days you normally study.

Note: Part-time education is defined as less than 16 hours a week.[124]

Part-time work [125]

To receive YPBA for any day, you must be available on that day to attend an interview for WBLYP or to take up a WBLYP place. The Jobcentre Plus guidance to staff defines part-time work as eight hours per week or less during the hours of 9 to 5 Monday to Friday. Weekend and evening work does not affect entitlement to YPBA.

You can get YPBA for any day when you work part-time and sign a statement saying that you are:

- willing to give up the employment to take up a training opportunity, and
- available to attend training interviews on the days you normally work.

Ending YPBA

The Jobcentre Plus office should notify you and the Connexions/Careers Service 20 days before the YPBA is due to end. When the last payment of YPBA is made, you will be sent a letter saying that it can no longer be paid. If relevant, it will give a future date when you can make a new application for YPBA.

YPBA will stop:[126]

- if you find work, start WBLYP, return to education, or become sick before the full 40-day period of entitlement is reached

- when 40 days' YPBA has been paid (unless you have a disability or health problem – see page 122)
- when a combined total of Extended Child Benefit and YPBA reach 40 days
- the day before the your 18th birthday is reached (unless you have a disability or health problem)
- when a claim for JSA under the Severe Hardship provision is successful
- if you enter e2e training
- if you cease to be registered for WBLYP with Connexions/Careers Service for any reason; or
- if you fail to attend the Jobcentre Plus office (for example, to sign on and you do not attend again within five working days).[127]

Refusal of a suitable Work-Based Learning for Young People (WBLYP) place

When you apply for YPBA, you must sign this declaration on form BA1:

'I understand that I must be prepared to accept an offer of a suitable place on Work-Based Learning for Young People, and that payment of Young Person's Bridging Allowance may be stopped if I refuse such an offer without good cause.'

The only circumstance in which your entitlement to YPBA should be questioned is if you refuse the offer of suitable WBLYP while you are receiving YPBA.[128]

Having been notified of a refusal of a WBLYP place by Connexions/Careers Service, the Jobcentre Plus office will refer your case to a Decision Maker (DM) for consideration of 'Refusal of Training'. Connexions/Careers Service will include in their report to the Jobcentre Plus office full details of the training offered and the reasons given for refusal.

The Decision Maker gives an 'opinion' on whether you would have been disallowed from receiving JSA if you were entitled to it, and can recommend that you be disqualified for between one and 26 weeks. In other words, the sanction regime for JSA is applied to YPBA .

These are the steps that will be taken if you refuse a suitable WBLYP place:[129]

- Connexions/Careers Service notifies Jobcentre Plus that you have refused to take up a WBLYP place without good cause. They will also include full details of the training offered and the reasons given for refusal.
- Jobcentre Plus will then suspend your YPBA.
- You will be invited to comment on the report of refusal of training (within 14 days).
- Papers are referred to an 'executive grade officer' at Jobcentre Plus to decide if the case is straightforward. If it is considered to be straightforward, you will be paid any arrears outstanding. If it is not, the case will be referred to the DM for 'opinion only'.

If the disallowance goes beyond the end of the YPBA period, the disallowance will be imposed to the end of the YPBA period. If you subsequently get a training place and leave it, you can still apply for YPBA again.

Appeals

There is no independent appeals procedure against disqualification, but you can appeal against the decision to the business manager of the Jobcentre Plus office.[130] Jobcentre Plus guidance states that you should appeal within 21 days,[131] but this rule has no legal basis to it and is less than the period allowed for social security appeals. However, it would be best to try and appeal within this time limit.

If you provide new information the appeal is referred back to the DM to review the original opinion. Otherwise the manager will decide whether or not to overturn the decision to disqualify you. Although DMs only give an 'opinion' in cases involving YPBA, they will still make their recommendation as if they were being asked to assess a claim for JSA.

You can also complain via your MP and in some cases, you may be able to take a type of legal action known as judicial review to challenge a decision to stop your YPBA or if the period of disqualification is too long (there is discretion about how long the period of disqualification should be and you can also challenge this point).

Requalifying for YPBA

Once you have been paid your full 40 days of YPBA (unless you have a disability) you can requalify for YPBA only if:

- you have left WBLYP or a job since last receiving YPBA; and
- it is more than 52 weeks from the first day for which YPBA was paid.

Leaving a job or WBLYP place only qualifies you for YPBA once. To requalify you would have to leave another job or WBLYP place.

If you have not got a WBLYP place or a job when your entitlement to YPBA ends and are left without an income you may apply for JSA under the severe hardship provisions (see page 46).

YPBA after work-based learning programme suspension [132]

If a suspension of work-based learning occurs, for example, due to an employer becoming insolvent, you can be treated under the WBLYP guarantee and may be eligible for YPBA.

It is possible that your work-based learning allowance or Education Maintenance Allowance will be stopped pending transfer to another suitable work-based learning place. In this case, you will become eligible for YPBA, provided it is outside the child benefit extension period and you have not received your full entitlement in the last 52 weeks.

If you had 'employee' status on a Modern Apprenticeship, and your employer's business ceased, you stay on the Modern Apprenticeship under the learning provider. The learning provider must then find you another employer and you are therefore not eligible for YPBA.

Social Fund Payments

The Social Fund is a system of grants and loans to help with one-off expenses. One part of the Social Fund consists of regulated payments for maternity, funerals and cold weather, the other of discretionary loans and grants made out of a fixed budget held by each local Jobcentre Plus office.

Grants do not have to be repaid.

Sure Start Maternity Grant [133]

This is a grant of £500 per baby which is paid if you are expecting a baby in the next 11 weeks or if you have given birth within the last 3 months, or if you are adopting a baby less than 12 months old. You must have written confirmation (which can be done on the claim form) from a health professional (for example, a midwife or health visitor) that you have had advice about the baby's health and welfare (or on maternal health if you claim before the baby is born).

You, or your partner, must also be getting one of the following benefits in the week that you make your claim:

* Income Support
* Income-based Jobseeker's Allowance
* Tax Credits (but only if you receive more than the family element of Child Tax Credit or you receive a disability or severe disability element in Working Tax Credit).

Any savings you have do not affect the grant. You will need to make a claim for the grant, because it is not paid automatically.

Funeral Payments

Claim on form SF200 if you are the nearest relative of the deceased, have to arrange the funeral and you are getting IS, JSA , HB or CTB.

Cold Weather Payment

Automatically payable to those in receipt of IS or Income-based JSA who are disabled or who have a disabled child or you have a child under 5. The amount payable is £8.50.

Community Care Grants

These are discretionary grants which you might get if you receive Income Support or Income-based Jobseeker's Allowance. This includes people who are in hospital or prison or similar accommodation and who are expected to receive those benefits within the next 6 weeks. Any capital above £500 that you may have will reduce the amount of grant you receive. You must also show that the grant will help in at least one of the following ways:[134]

- Help you or someone you claim benefit for to re-establish in the community after being in institutional or residential care (e.g. prison, hospital, care home, foster parents)
- Help you or someone you claim for to stay living in the community rather than risk entering institutional care
- Ease exceptional pressure on you and your family (e.g. to meet the extra one-off costs of having a disabled child)
- Help you to set up home as part of a resettlement plan after being homeless
- Help with travel and reasonable overnight costs to visit someone in hospital or residential care, or
- Allow you to care for a prisoner who has been released on temporary licence.

People setting themselves up in their own accommodation should submit a list to the Social Fund Officer of all the things that they need, priced from something like an Argos catalogue. The 'normal' payment is usually around £500-£700 but that isn't fixed in law and you could get more if you can show what essential items you need.

If you are leaving care, you can usually get a grant from the local council that looked after you but that doesn't stop you from getting a community care grant if you meet the rules above and still need essential items.

Because these grants are discretionary it often helps to have evidence and supporting letters to help your claim. Don't be put off from claiming and if you are refused, you can ask a Social Fund Inspector to review your case.

Crisis Loans [135]

These discretionary loans are for anyone who doesn't have enough money to meet their immediate short-term needs and who needs help because of an emergency or a disaster, especially if it is the only way to prevent serious damage or risk to their health. The most common crisis loan payment is to cover the first few weeks of a JSA or IS claim, when it is taking a while to get your normal weekly benefit sorted out. But remember that this is money that has to be paid back out of your benefit when you get it. Payments can also be made for rent in advance to a private landlord if you are also getting a Community Care Grant after being in institutional care.

If your crisis loan application indicates that your circumstances mean that you may qualify for a Community Care Grant, the DWP officer dealing with the claim should consider whether or not you qualify for a Community Care Grant;[136] however, you cannot rely on this always being done.

If you have had a JSA sanction applied (see page 54), you can only get a Crisis Loan in restricted circumstances.

There is a list of excluded items for which you can't get either a Community Care Grant or a Crisis Loan. These include:

- Education or training needs (including school clothing or uniform);
- Medical, surgical or dental items or services;
- Debts to government departments;
- Work-related expenses.

In addition, Crisis Loans cannot be made for:

- Telephone costs;
- Mobility needs;
- Holidays;
- Television or radio costs;
- Mobility needs;
- Motor vehicle expenses (except travel costs).

You can apply for a Crisis Loan by telephone, but if you are at a DWP office, staff have been instructed not to send you home to make a phone call[137] and if you have difficulty being understood on the phone or if English is not your first language, you should be offered an immediate office interview.[138]

Budgeting Loans

To get a Budgeting Loan, you must have been getting either Income Support or Income-based Jobseeker's Allowance for at least 26 weeks. Any capital you have over £1000 will reduce the amount of loan you receive.

The loan must be needed for at least one of the following:

- Furniture and household equipment
- Clothing and footwear
- Rent in advance and/or removal costs
- Home improvements, maintenance and repairs
- Travel costs
- Expenses to do with looking for or taking up work
- Debts for any of the above.

If a loan is refused you can ask for a review by a Social Fund Inspector. You will have to repay both Crisis and Budgeting Loans but you can ask for the amount being taken out of your benefit for repayment to be reduced and for the loan to then be repaid over a longer period. It is possible for the DWP to waive recovery particularly if your circumstances change for the worse after you apply for the loan.[139] However, they may resist waiving recovery even though the law clearly confers a discretion. Seek advice. Loan repayments can also be 'rescheduled' over a longer period, meaning that the amount deducted from your benefits is reduced, though it will take longer to repay the loan. Both budgeting and crisis loans are interest free.

When considering whether or not to make a discretionary Social Fund loan or grant, DWP officials must consider the following:

- The nature, extent and urgency of the need
- The existence of resources from which the need may be met
- The possibility that some other person or body may wholly or partly meet it
- Where the payment is repayable, the likelihood of repayment and the time within which repayment is likely
- The total amount of the local Social Fund budget.[140]

Because you can be refused a Crisis or a Budgeting Loan on the grounds that you are unlikely to be able to repay it, if you need a crisis loan because your benefit has not yet been paid, you can ask for an interim payment of the benefit[141] or you can argue that you are more likely than not to receive benefit and will then be able to repay.[142]

You should also apply for a Community Care Grant in preference to any loan – you are entitled to apply for both.

Endnotes

1   S 8 (2) Tax Credits Act 2002 & Reg 3 (1) Child Tax Credit Regulations 2002

2   Reg 5 The Child Benefit (General) Regulations 2006

3   Reg 5 (2) (f) The Child Benefit (General) Regulations 2006

4   Reg 3 The Child Benefit (General) Regulations 2006

5   S 141 Social Security Contributions and Benefits Act 1992 as amended by S 1 Child Benefit Act 2005

6   Reg 3 Child Benefit (General) Regulations 2006

7   Reg 1 (3) The Child Benefit (General) Regulations 2006

8   Reg 3 (2) The Child Benefit (General) Regulations 2006

9   Reg 1 (3) The Child Benefit (General) Regulations 2006

10 Reg 3 (4) The Child Benefit (General) Regulations 2006

11 Reg2 (5) The Child Benefit (General) Regulations 2006

12 Reg 6 (3) The Child Benefit (General) Regulations 2006

13 Reg 6 (4) The Child Benefit (General) Regulations 2006

14 S 8 (4) Tax Credits Act 2002, Regs 2 and 5(1) – (3A) Child Tax Credit Regulations

15 Jobcentre Plus JSA for 16-17 year olds Guidance. Initial contact section, paras 2-3.

16 R(SB) 8/85 & R(SB) 4/83

17 S 3A(1) (e) Jobseekers Act 1995

18 S 3A (1) (d) Jobseekers Act 1995

19 Reg 4 ZA & sch 1B Income Support (General) Regulations 1987

20 Regs 13 (2) (a) – (e) Income Support (General) Regulations 1987 (as amended from 10th April 2006)

21 DMG Vol 4 Ch 20 20668

22 DMG, Vol 4, para 20670 – 20675 and Reg 13(3) (a) Income Support (General) Regulations 1987

23 DMG Vol 4, para 20669

24 DMG, Vol 4, para 20693

25 Kelly v Monklands District Council 1866 SLT 169

26 R(IS) 9/94

27 R(SB) 2/87

28 DMG, Vol 4, para 20690

29 R(SB) 2/87

30 CIS/4096/2005

31 IS Bulletin 04-07 Estranged Young People aged 16 - 19 claiming Income Support.

32 DMG, Vol 4, para 20694

33 R(IS) 9/94

34 Reg 57 (2) Jobseeker's Allowance Regulations 1986

35 Reg 60 Jobseeker's Allowance Regulations 1986

36 Reg 61 Jobseeker's Allowance Regulations 1986

37 S 16 (1) Jobseeker's Act 1995

38 Jobcentre Plus internal staff guidance on Jobseeker's Allowance for 16/17 year olds ("JSA Guidance") : Initial Contact

39 JSA Guidance :Initial contact para 35

40 JSA Guidance :Initial contact para 6

41 JSA Guidance :Initial contact para 28

42 Reg 2 Social Security (Payments on Account, Overpayments and Recovery) Regulations 1988

43 JSA Guidance: New Jobseeker Interview para 1

44 JSA Guidance: New Jobseeker Interview para 7

45 JSA Guidance: New Jobseeker Interview para 25

46 JSA Guidance: New Jobseeker Interview para 23

47 JSA Guidance: New Jobseeker Interview para 65

48 Reg 64 (2) & (3) Jobseeker's Allowance Regulations 1986

49 Reg 65 Jobseeker's Allowance Regulations 1986

50 Reg 65 (2) Jobseeker's Allowance Regulations 1986

51 Reg 65 (5) Jobseeker's Allowance Regulations 1986

52 JSA Guidance: Labour Market Issues: para 84

53 S 16 (1) (a) Jobseekers Act 1995

54 JSA Guidance: Making a severe hardship decision: para 208

55 JSA Guidance: Making a severe hardship decision: para 209 -210

56 JSA Guidance: Making a severe hardship decision: para 83

57 JSA Guidance: Making a severe hardship decision: para 87

58 JSA Guidance: Making a severe hardship decision: para 5

59 JSA Guidance: Making a severe hardship decision: para 6 -8

60 JSA Guidance: Making a severe hardship decision: para 11

61 JSA Guidance: Making a severe hardship decision: para 10

62 JSA Guidance: Making a severe hardship decision: para 18

63 JSA Guidance: Making a severe hardship decision: para 29 & 36

64 JSA Guidance: Conducting a severe hardship interview: paras 43-53

65 JSA Guidance: Conducting a severe hardship interview: para 59

66 JSA Guidance: Conducting a severe hardship interview: paras 60-79

67 JSA Guidance: Making a severe hardship decision: paras 127-134

68 JSA Guidance: Making a severe hardship decision: paras 33-100

69 Reg 27 Jobseeker's Allowance Regulations 1996

70 Reg 67 (3) Jobseeker's Allowance Regulations 1996

71 Reg 67 (1) & (2) Jobseeker's Allowance Regulations 1996

72 JSA Guidance: Labour market issues: para 12

73 JSA Guidance: Labour market issues: para 24

74 JSA Guidance: Labour market issues: paras 123–125. Also see DWP Decision Maker's Guide. Vol 6 para 34766 et seq

75 DWP Decision Maker's Guide. Vol 6 para 34769

76 JSA Guidance: Labour market issues: para 125

77 DWP Decision Maker's Guide. Vol 6 para 34797

78 DWP Decision Maker's Guide. Vol 6 para 34799

79 DWP Decision Maker's Guide. Vol 6 para 34780

80 DWP Decision Maker's Guide. Vol 6 para 34811

81 DWP Decision Maker's Guide. Vol 6 para 34757

82 Summarised in DWP Decision Maker's Guide. Vol 6 para 34002 and reflecting several pieces of legislation

83 R(U) 8/74

84 S 20(3) Jobseekers Act 1995 & reg 74 Jobseeker's Allowance Regulations 1996

85 Para 155 et seq. Benefits Liaison Instructions and Good Practice Guidelines for Connexions Services. DfES

86 S16 (2) (b) Jobseekers Act 1995

87 JSA Guidance: Labour market issues: para53

[88] R (U) 2/77

[89] DWP Decision Maker's Guide. Vol 6 Para 34106

[90] R (U) 10/53

[91] R (U) 3/81

[92] Reg 71 Jobseeker's Allowance Regulations 1996

[93] R (U) 25/52

[94] DWP Decision Maker's Guide. Vol 6, Chapter 34 para 34278 et seq

[95] DWP Decision Maker's Guide. Vol 6, Chapter 35.

[96] Para 139 et seq. Benefits Liaison Instructions and Good Practice Guidelines for Connexions Services. DfES.

[97] Jobcentre Plus: Allowances Payments Guide. Chapter 4 ("JC+ APG"): Para 12

[98] JC+ APG: Para: 143

[99] JC+ APG: Para 12

[100] JC+ APG: Para 12

[101] JC+ APG: Para 133

[102] JC+ APG: Para 42

[103] JC+ APG: Para 46

[104] JC+ APG: Para 34

[105] JC+ APG: Para 181

[106] JC+ APG: Para 182

[107] JC+ APG: Para 183

[108] JC+ APG: Para 17

[109] JC+ APG: Para 30

[110] JC+ APG: Para 18

[111] JC+ APG: Para 20

[112] JC+ APG: Para 29

[113] JC+ APG: Para 174

[114] JC+ APG: Para 177

[115] JC+ APG: Paras 54 & 88

[116] JC+ APG: Para 58

[117] JC+ APG: Para 56

[118] JC+ APG: Para 65

[119] JC+ APG: Para 173

[120] JC+ APG: Para 165

[121] JC+ APG: Para 168

[122] JC+ APG: Paras 123 - 4

[123] JC+ APG: Para 125

[124] JC+ APG: Para 146

[125] JC+ APG: Para 143 - 5

[126] JC+ APG: Para 120

[127] JC+ APG: Para 140

[128] JC+ APG: Para 193

[129] JC+ APG: Para 194

[130] JC+ APG: Para 209

[131] JC+ APG: Appendix 7

[132] JC+ APG: Paras 162 - 4

[133] Reg 5 Social Fund Maternity and Funeral Expenses (General) Regulations 1987

[134] Social Fund Directions. Direction 4.

[135] Social Fund Directions No's 23 & 29

[136] Social Fund Directions: No 49

[137] DWP staff guidance on Crisis Loans: Paragraph 29

[138] DWP staff guidance on Crisis Loans: Paragraph 24

[139] See use of the word "repayable" in S.139 (3) Social Security Contributions and Benefits Act 1992 & Social Fund Direction No 5

[140] S.140 (1) Social Security Contributions and Benefits Act 1992

[141] Reg 2 Social Security (Payments on Account, etc) Regs 1988

[142] Social Fund Commissioner's Advice on Amounts to Award: (Living Expenses) Effective from 04/02/02

4 Financial support for young people remaining in learning

Your choices

This part of the Guide describes what you can do when you leave full-time compulsory education at the age of 16. Broadly you have the choice of

- staying in learning as a full-time student, where you might follow a traditional learning programme
- staying in learning, where you might learn a trade by following something like a Modern Apprenticeship
- getting a job
- not doing anything.

To help you think about the future, an understanding of the following basic facts may help you to decide what to do.

Financial help

As a 16-18 year old you will be entitled to free education, where all the costs of learning programmes are met by the state.[1] In addition, you might get some financial assistance to help you stay in learning. For example, if you decide to

- stay in learning as a full-time student, where you might follow a traditional learning programme in a school sixth form or at a FE College you might be eligible to receive an Education Maintenance Allowance. You may also qualify for help with expenses such as to cover the costs of childcare, travel and the purchase of materials you need for the course.

- stay in learning to learn a trade by following something like a Modern Apprenticeship you will receive a training allowance of at least £40 a week if you do not have employed status. If you do have employed status you will be paid a wage. You may also qualify for help with expenses such as to cover the costs of childcare, travel and the purchase of learning materials.

The impact of qualifications

The qualifications you possess will have an impact on what work you can do and the amount of money you can earn, now and in the future. There is a large body of evidence to show that people with no or few qualifications have more trouble finding work and have a lower earning potential. So you should be aware that qualification levels relate to what you will be able to earn in the future.

For example, it is generally accepted that the majority of people leaving school at age 16 will be qualified to level 2 because they will have achieved 5 GCSEs graded between grades A to C. Given that many employers will look for more qualifications than this, it is highly likely that

- you will find it difficult to get a job
- your choices of jobs will be severely limited
- you will be on a low wage with limited opportunity for progression.

Then there are those young people who leave compulsory education without having achieved any qualifications at all. For these young people, getting a well-paid job is even more difficult.

Then there are those who choose not to stay in learning or take a job with training and therefore do nothing. Maybe you feel like 'dropping out' or simply wouldn't mind a break for a while after leaving school. Often those who intended to go back to learning to give themselves better chances in life never actually do. The longer you leave it, the harder it becomes to go back.

It is worth noting here that the Government will not fund you to continue in education to achieve qualifications above level 2 once you are over the age of 19, except in exceptional circumstances. This means that you will effectively miss your chance of free education and you could find your employment options severely limited in the future.

In addition, if you do not take part in learning at this stage in your life, you may have to go back to learning when you are older in order to get a range of qualifications that will help you secure a better future. This could mean you will have to pay for courses out of your own pocket and do them at times when you would rather be doing something else. So you would be well advised to think about what you should be doing at this stage in your life so that you take advantage of what is currently on offer.

If you do stay in some kind of learning or training be aware that the decisions you make now can have an impact on what you end up doing for a living in the future. Deciding which learning route to take is important.

The different routes

The traditional routes

If you choose to stay in learning as a full-time student, where you might follow a traditional learning programme, you may

- stay on at school and enter the sixth form
- go to a sixth-form college
- go to a FE college
- go to a private training organisation

where you could

- retake your GCSEs or switch to vocational GCSEs
- study a range of academic subjects including General Certificates in Education (GCEs), which are commonly known as As or A levels and/ or Vocational Certificates in Education (VCEs), which are commonly known as vocational 'A' levels
- follow a single vocational course where you might complete a National Diploma, National Certificate or other vocational qualification offered by an organisation such as Edexcel or City and Guilds.

Going into Modern Apprenticeships

If you choose to stay in learning but would prefer to follow a vocational framework, you could go to

- a FE college
- a work-based learning provider

where, depending on your ability, you could enrol on:

- an Entry to Employment programme
- a Foundation Modern Apprenticeship programme
- an Advanced Modern Apprenticeship programme.

Getting a job

If you decide to find a job, you could

- do voluntary work
- go abroad to work
- get a job with training
- get a job where training is not provided
- become self-employed.

Doing a job and getting training

It is worth noting here that if you choose to get a job you may still be involved in training where you learn and develop your knowledge and skills. This is because your employer might:

- allow you time off for day release at a local college to study for a vocational qualification
- offer you a place on a Foundation or Advanced Modern Apprenticeship programme, that they may run on their own or with the help of a local FE College or work-based learning provider.

The right to time off for study or training

In any case you would be wise to know that since 1st September 1999, employees who are aged 16 or 17, are not in full-time education, and are not qualified to level 2 (see page 91) have the right to paid time off work to study or train for approved qualifications. The aim is to help these young employees to get the skills and qualifications they need, and to help businesses to be more competitive.

You can do your studying or training in the workplace, on the job or elsewhere on your employer's premises, or it could take place in a FE College, with an approved training provider, or through open or distance learning. The time you take to study or train will be what is considered reasonable, after taking into account the requirements of the course/ training programme and the effect you might have on your employer's business by having the time off from work.

You are entitled to receive payment for the time you spend on training at your normal hourly rate. Where an employer unreasonably refuses to permit time off, or fails to pay you the payment to which you are entitled, you can present a complaint to an Employment Tribunal.

Getting careers advice

As you see from the list of options above, you do have quite a wide range of choices. You may think that doing a Modern Apprenticeship would appeal to you or perhaps you would like to carry on studying for academic qualifications. But before you make a decision you should consult a Connexions adviser who can give you more information about your options. Your adviser will tell you about what qualifications or attributes you need to have to get on to the learning programme of your choice, and what you will get out of taking this particular route.

The Connexions Service has been established to help you achieve your full potential. You can access and use the service on a purely voluntary basis and Connexions staff fully appreciate that their impartiality and confidentiality are the primary reasons why people like you use the service for advice and guidance.

When you make contact with Connexions, the personal adviser will need some basic information so that they can help you. This basic information will be your contact details and information about how you have progressed through learning.

Further guidance on the role of the Connexions Service is provided in Chapter 2

Making decisions

But whatever you decide to do the choice you make should be based on your abilities, and what you want to do, your aptitudes and aspirations. This is important because lots of young people start a learning programme that does not really suit them. They get bored and leave the learning programme. All sorts of pressures often force young people into doing something that they really do not want to do. Some young people are better at academic study than others. If you find studying traditional subjects difficult then do more practical subjects. Tell the Connexions or Careers adviser what you want to do and talk about your strengths and weaknesses. It is essential that you join a programme that suits the way you like to learn. Also think about where you want to learn: some people are more suited to a FE College than others.

What follows is more information about how the different learning programmes are delivered. This information should help you to decide which type of learning programme would suit you best.

Following a traditional learning route

If you choose to stay in learning as a full-time student, where you might follow a traditional learning programme, your study options are likely to fall into one of the following three headings:

- GCEs – General Certificate of Education. This group of qualifications are more commonly known as 'A' levels.
- VCEs – Vocational Certificate of Education. This group of qualifications are known as vocational 'A' levels
- Other traditional vocational qualifications such as those offered by Edexcel, City and Guilds and OCR.

School-based qualifications

The courses on offer at school are predominantly AS or A Levels and GCSE retakes after the age of sixteen.

A lot of people think about retaking their GCSE's and usually only resit English and Maths. Students tend to do this in the autumn term alongside other courses of study. If you're thinking about doing retakes, it would be a good idea to speak directly to the school to check availability.

Further Education

The courses on offer are AS, A Levels, AVCEs, GNVQs, BTECs, NVQs, City and Guilds, and Apprenticeships. You can apply for any course after you are sixteen years of age.

Financial support

If you are a school leaver between the ages of 16 and 18 you will not have to pay for your college course.

A Learner Support Fund can help with things like transport, childcare, books and equipment. There are even schemes that can help with accommodation costs if it's essential for you move closer to a specialist college. For full details on eligibility and information on what you can use the fund for, visit the website. The link is:
http://www.support4learning.org.uk/home/index.cfm

The Education Maintenance Allowance (EMA) scheme is also available and encourages young people between the ages of 16 and 19 to stay on at further education. Students studying any course up to and including A Levels can earn up to £30 per week.

You will be eligible to claim the allowance if your parents' or guardian's income is less than £30,000 per year. You can use the extra money for anything you want: driving lessons, travel or food, for example.

All you have to do is turn up for lessons regularly, sign a contract with your college detailing what's expected of you and be able to show how you are progressing over the course of the year. If you are interested in applying for EMA, you can call the free EMA helpline on 080 810 16219 or visit the website. The link is: www.direct.gov.uk/ema

Although information on all of the funding schemes open to you should be provided by your school or college or the education department of your local council, you can also speak to a personal adviser at Connexions Direct.

See also page 104.

Some facts about General Certificates of Education (GCEs)

How are GCEs organised?

General Certificates in Education are available in over 40 different subject areas.

Each GCE is divided into two levels – AS and A2 levels. AS exams are typically taken at the end of the first year of advanced study and lead to qualifications in their own right. AS qualifications count towards the first half of a full A level qualification. This means that at the end of the first year of a two-year study programme you are awarded an AS certificate as recognition of what you have achieved so far and then you go on studying for another year to be awarded the A level.

Do you need entry qualifications?

Normally you will need 5 GCSEs at grade C or above to do a full-time GCE course. Mature students may be accepted without the normal entry qualifications.

Where do learners study?

GCEs are available in school sixth forms, sixth-form colleges and FE Colleges. Where you study your course will depend on what is available locally. You would be well advised to choose a centre that offers other courses because you may also want to study other qualifications such as VCEs.

How are GCEs assessed and graded?

These qualifications are assessed through a combination of external examination and/or coursework. The level of demand for an AS is that expected of candidates half way through a full Advanced Level course of study. Therefore as you gain more knowledge, the second half of the GCE is assessed at a higher standard.

You will also have to take a demanding final assessment, which draws together material from across the whole course. This is designed to show your understanding of how everything you have learned fits together.

Awards will be made on an A-E grading scale and students failing to meet the minimum standard for an award are recorded as 'unclassified'.

Where do GCEs lead?

AS and A levels are widely recognised by employers and universities. They provide the traditional route into University degree courses.

Some facts about Vocational Certificates of Education (VCEs)

What is the purpose of VCEs?

Known as vocational A levels, these qualifications enable you to develop skills, knowledge and understanding of vocational areas. They can help you prepare for both the world of work and progress to Higher Education.

What would you learn?

They allow you to gain experience of industry and commerce. You will spend time completing work-related assignments, where you may work with local employers to learn more about an area of work such as business, leisure and recreation, travel and tourism or engineering. As you do the assignments you will be encouraged to develop other skills that are valuable in any job, such as communication, numeracy and the use of information technology.

How will VCEs help you?

The knowledge and skills you gain by taking a VCE will:

- prepare you for employment
- allow you entry into further and higher education.

How are VCEs organised?

The qualifications are made up of units. These units allow the qualifications to be available in the following three different sizes:

- Advanced Subsidiary, where you are required to take three units.
- Advanced Level, where you are required to take six units.
- Double Award, where you are required to take 12 units.

Who they are for?

VCEs are aimed at 16 to 19 year olds, but some adults who are returning to learning also do them.

Where do learners study?

VCEs are available in school sixth forms, sixth-form colleges and FE Colleges. Where you study your course will depend on what is available locally. You would be well advised to choose a centre that offers other courses because you may also want to study other qualifications such as GCEs.

How will you study?

You will be involved in planning your own learning activities, where you will be required to work alone and in groups, spend time out of the classroom visiting employers and other organisations, solving problems and meeting deadlines.

You spend much of your time working on assignments and projects. For example, if you are doing business studies you might be asked to research, develop and present a marketing plan for a new product

What subjects are available?

The range of areas can include Art & Design, Business, Construction and the Built Environment, Engineering, Health & Social Care, Hospitality and Catering, Information and Communication Technology, Leisure and Recreation, Manufacturing and so on. New areas are being developed all the time to cover wider areas of the economy.

How will you be assessed?

Your work will be assessed through a combination of coursework and tests and each unit is certificated so if you don't complete the full qualification you will still receive recognition for the units you did achieve.

What are your employment options?

If you want to get a job after school or college and have a good idea of the area you wish to work in then you should look very closely at taking a VCE alongside your other subjects because many companies recruit students who have taken a vocational course. This is because employers increasingly value the work skills and vocational knowledge that learners gain on these programmes. However, they may also expect a range of other qualifications including GCSEs and GCEs,

Some facts about traditional vocational qualifications

Traditional vocational qualifications require you to follow a course structure that includes more conventional methods of learning. These awards retain the emphasis on developing practical skills and knowledge, but they tend to be classroom-based with assessment by written and practical examinations. These qualifications are usually recognised by certificates and diplomas. The content of these programmes and how they will be assessed will depend on the awarding body offering them. For example, some awarding bodies require you to complete assignments and case studies that are marked by an external examiner as well as taking examinations. The number and range of vocational qualifications on offer is huge and covers a wide range of jobs. For example you could do a course that gives you the knowledge and skills you need to work in a science-based industry, the care sector, in engineering, design, the performing arts, public services, the sports industry, sports, exercise and leisure sector or travel & tourism.

What are the progression routes?

These types of qualifications often offer good progression routes where you might start on an introductory or foundation programme and then move up to higher awards. The higher-level qualifications are often recognised by Universities and allow people to progress onto a degree course.

The differences between these full-time study programmes

The main difference between GCEs/VCEs and traditional vocational qualifications is the number of subjects you will study. For example if you take

- GCEs you may study English, English Literature, Geography and History
- VCEs you might study Art & Design, Business and Hospitality & Catering

With traditional vocational qualifications you would concentrate on one area where you might study carpentry, or motor mechanics, or maintenance engineering, or hairdressing or animal care.

It is also worth noting here that there is nothing stopping you from doing a couple of GCEs and a VCE. If you get a job with training you could well follow one of the traditional vocational qualifications, because your employer may offer you day release to develop the knowledge and skills you need to do your job.

Higher Education

Depending on the course you choose, there are four types of HE qualification:

- Honours degree – either Bachelor of Arts (BA) or Bachelor of Science (BSc).
- Foundation Degree – for learning practical skills for a specific job in a specific industry (e.g. Hotel Management, Aircraft Engineering, Journalism).
- Sandwich course – a degree course which includes one year working in industry or a year abroad.
- Higher National Diploma (HND) or Diploma of Higher Education – qualifications that focus on a particular kind of job. They can be topped up into a full degree later.

Higher Education is the phase of education that happens after you leave school or college at eighteen and offers you a range of advanced courses and qualifications. At this level, you usually study just one or two subjects: either 'classic' subjects like Art, History, or English literature, or newer, modern courses such as Sports Science, Music Production, or Multimedia Programming.

Financial support

Continuing in education after the age of nineteen can be expensive but investing in your future should be worthwhile. Carrying out some research into the options available will help you to ease any worries.

What follows are some ways in which you may consider getting funding to continue your studies.

The main options are:

- Loans – there is a Student Loans Company owned by the Government which provides a loan to cover your living costs and part of your tuition fees. You are expected to pay it back, but not until after you graduate and are earning a certain amount of money. This is a link to the Loans Company: www.slc.co.uk

- Sponsorship – this option is to find a company that will sponsor your studies, but bear in mind that the competition is steep. As well as getting your tuition fees (and sometimes your living costs) paid for, you are usually guaranteed a job once you get your degree. If you have a particular career in mind, research companies in that field and find out if they offer any sponsorship programmes. To search for scholarships visit the hot courses website. The link is: http://www.studentmoney.org/

More information on student finance is available on the Aim Higher website. The link is: http://www.aimhigher.ac.uk/student_finance/index.cfm

Structure and settings

Seminars and lectures are not lessons as such, but provide support and guidance for your own reading. You will need to manage your time effectively, particularly if you are going to meet deadlines, as well as developing new academic skills for tasks such as writing essays. These techniques are developed over time, but lots of help is available. For tips on how to get the most out of lectures visit the StudentUK website. The link is: http://www.studentuk.com/

Each university is different, but most places will have clubs and societies for all popular recreations and interests. 'Raising and Giving' (RAG) societies are often busy on campus all year, organising stunts and fundraising for good causes. The major political parties usually have student branches also. Cultural, religious and faith group societies are available. To get more of an idea of the types of clubs visit the Student Zone Clubs and Societies Directory. The link is: www.studentzone.org.uk/ents/clubs.html

Moving out

When you choose university, you don't just have to think about your course and finances, you also have to think about where you're going to live if you have decided to move away from home.

Most universities have accommodation on campus or nearby, either Halls of Residence or privately-run housing. In August and September each year, lots of students are going to be looking for accommodation, so as soon as your place on your course is confirmed, you need to sort out accommodation. Most first-year students choose to live in halls on campus or in university-managed accommodation, as it's easy to meet people, safer and you will not have bills to worry about.

After the first year you may decide to rent a house with your friends. This can be lots of fun, but you'll need to learn to live with other people and to budget as a group.

Education Maintenance Allowances (EMAs)

Most young people will be able to get EMA for two or three years depending on how long they need to finish their studies. EMAs are ignored as income for benefits and tax credit purposes. See Chapter 1 for more information on EMAs.

Work-based learning

A few essential facts you need to know about work-based learning:

- Work-based learning lets you earn while you learn.
- Courses are designed to fit around your and your employer's needs.
- You can learn skills that are essential to your future career, such as computer literacy, communication skills, teamwork and how to meet deadlines.

- There are lots of qualifications available to you while you're working, including Foundation Degrees, Apprenticeships and Entry to Employment.

To find out more, try searching the web, calling your local university or college, or looking in local newspapers and trade magazines.

More information can be obtained from the Direct Government website. The link is: http://www.direct.gov.uk/en/EducationAndLearning/AdultLearning/TrainingAndWorkplaceLearning/DG_4001344

Going into Modern Apprenticeships

If you choose to stay in learning in order to learn a trade you could follow a Modern Apprenticeship, which is based on a framework of learning.

A vocational framework is where a number of essential learning elements have been brought together to create an integrated learning programme. For example, if you were to enrol on a Foundation Modern Apprenticeship you would follow a programme that helps you to develop:

- your personal skills
- your communication, numeracy and information technology skills
- the knowledge and skills needed to do a job in a particular vocational area
- occupational competence.

So instead of simply following a number of subjects you go on a programme that has been specifically designed to meet the requirements of a particular sector/industry.

There are currently three learning programmes that are organised as vocational frameworks and are as follows:

- Entry to Employment.
- Foundation Modern Apprenticeship.
- Advanced Modern Apprenticeship.

What follows is more guidance on how the different learning programmes are delivered. This information should help you decide if this type of learning programme would suit you.

Entry to Employment (e2e)

What is e2e?

e2e is a learning programme that aims to help those young people who are aged 16 to 18 who are not ready or able to enter directly Modern Apprenticeship programmes, further education or employment. Young people are given the skills they will need to prepare for progression to employment, employment with training, a Modern Apprenticeship programme or further education.

The programme is not:

- time bound
- specified in terms of guided learning hours or attendance, but you do have to meet the minimum requirements
- qualification driven but you may want to get qualifications to help you progress and develop
- prescriptive, and learning providers have developed a range of options to suit the needs of the individual learner.

Am I eligible for e2e?

You are eligible if you are aged 16 to 18 years old, live in England, are not participating in any form of post-16 learning and need help to progress to further learning and/or a job.

Young people under the Extended Guarantee can also participate in e2e. This means that older young people can be admitted at the discretion of the local LSC, provided the young person is not eligible for New Deal and their programme of learning can be completed by their 25th birthday.

Who is e2e for?

e2e is primarily aimed at young people who are not ready to enter training, employment or further education. Young people who take up e2e will have a wide variety of aptitudes and abilities. Broadly speaking, young people who are likely to benefit from e2e programmes are those

- with significant learning difficulties and/or disabilities
- who are currently not engaged in any form of learning and may have had a negative experience of school
- who may have one or more barriers to overcome such as alcohol abuse, drug abuse, depression or homelessness.

How do I enrol on e2e?

Staff from local Connexions Services will advise you about e2e opportunities within your local area. Connexions staff will refer you to e2e if this is appropriate, as will other agencies such as Social Services or youth offending teams. Work-based learning providers can also identify young people who may benefit from e2e learning programmes. Your Connexions adviser is key to getting you on to an e2e programme even if you refer yourself to an e2e programme or are advised to apply by a local learning provider.

Your Connexions adviser will confirm that e2e is appropriate by carrying out an assessment, planning, implementation and review with you. This process is commonly known as the APIR. The APIR provides your Personal Adviser with guidance and a structure on how to work with you. It is used to assess your needs and identify your goals so that a personal action plan can be developed and implemented. The personal action plan will identify your learning and support needs and should be detailed on a Personal Adviser Referral Form. Your learning needs are those skills, knowledge and competences that you will need to acquire in order to help you fulfil your aims and aspirations. Your support needs are the additional help you will need in order to address and overcome any barriers that you may have to full participation in learning or work.

The information about you on the Personal Adviser Referral Form is then used to inform what you will do on e2e, which is then agreed and described on your e2e passport.

How long does e2e last?

e2e is not a time-bound learning programme because it is based on the needs of each individual. It has been recognised that there can be no 'quick-fix' for many of the young people who will enter e2e. Some young people prepare for entry to a Modern Apprenticeship, employment or further vocational learning opportunities in a very short time. Others will require much longer periods before they are ready to enter and sustain suitable training and employment if they have more complex personal and social needs.

How many hours per week will I have to spend on e2e?

This depends on your individual needs, but it is envisaged that you will attend somewhere between 16 and 40 hours per week. In exceptional circumstances attendance for 8-16 hours may be agreed by the local LSC.

Will I be given any financial support?

For details on allowances see Chapter 1 on EMAs. In addition, expenses are met in full. You will also get bonuses for starting e2e and for positive outcomes such as completing your Individual Activity Plan, the distance you have travelled in terms of how much you have progressed and developed, or if you gain qualifications.

The Individual Activity Plan describes the particular mix of activities that have been identified to meet your particular requirements. Your individual Development and Learning Plan is agreed by you, Connexions staff and the learning provider and is recorded on standard forms that are available in the e2e Passport. The e2e Passport is used to record and review what happens as you progress through the e2e programme.

What will I learn whilst on e2e?

The aim of e2e is to help you to

- improve your motivation and confidence
- develop your basic and/or key skills (see pages 114)

- develop personal effectiveness
- acquire knowledge, skills and understanding by sampling different work and learning contexts.

By the end of an e2e programme you should have developed

- vocational knowledge and understanding
- up-to-date work-related skills
- complementary knowledge and understanding beyond the vocational areas
- career awareness and career management skills
- your skills in
    - communication, numeracy, ICT
    - effective thinking, enterprise, problem solving
    - interpersonal relations and team working
    - citizenship.

How will I know what I need to develop?

There is an intensive period of initial assessment within e2e in order to identify clearly your individual learning and support needs. This might last between two and eight weeks depending on your individual needs. Learning providers offering e2e programmes are being encouraged to develop imaginative ways of organising these periods of initial assessment. The aim is to use the period of initial assessment to help young people develop their personal and social skills.

The arrangements for meeting your own learning and support needs will be set out in a document called the e2e Passport. This passport forms your overall plan, to which the different partners involved in delivering e2e can contribute. But if it is to be a useful plan your proactive involvement and commitment are essential. The passport aims to facilitate seamless transition from Connexions and to share information with e2e providers. The passport will integrate and provide a record of the key processes of initial assessment, planning individual learning and progress review.

The passport is made up of the following documents:

- **Personal Adviser Referral Form**

Your Connexions Personal Adviser will use this form when referring you to e2e.

- **Initial Assessment Summary**

Your e2e provider will use this form to provide a summary of your starting point on the programme, so that a simple benchmark can be agreed by which the distance you progress through the programme can be measured. It will help to set your key objectives that will be used to identify your individual e2e Programme.

- **e2e Programme**

This will identify the components of your e2e programme and anticipated accredited and non-accredited learning outcomes. Through regular updating, it will also serve as a simple record of what you have done and what you have achieved.

- **e2e Activity Plan and Review**

This supports the implementation of your e2e programme and provides a record of your progress. It is designed to cover a short time period and you will collect a number of these depending on the length of time you spend on e2e. You will need to constantly refer to this document, as it will provide a timetable of your planned activities along with their short-term targets and space for you to record comments about your learning. The document encourages you to review what you have done so that you can learn your lessons.

How is the learning programme structured?

All learners will undertake learning in the following three interdependent core areas:

- Basic and Key Skills
- Vocational development

- Personal and social development.

The extent of learning required within each of the core areas will be dictated by your needs and introduced at the most appropriate point. For example, learners with complex emotional and social needs may not be ready to undertake vocational learning until these needs have begun to be addressed.

Each core area is supported by a range of learning options supported by schemes of work at different levels from which you are able to select appropriate options.

Where and how will learning take place?

Learning takes place in a range of indoor and outdoor settings, using a range of different methods. These include class room type activities, one-to-one coaching, group activities, discussions, projects, presentations from speakers, on-line e-learning, open learning, work placements and experience, external visits, outward bound activities and volunteering.

Will I have to work towards qualifications?

Ideally, you will, wherever possible, work towards some form of qualification, recognising the fact that acquiring a qualification can be a powerful motivator to continue learning. However, within e2e there is flexibility in the range of qualifications that you can acquire. You may take national qualifications and others such as first aid courses, CLAIT, ECDL, or the City and Guilds Profile of Achievement.

What role do local support agencies such as youth offending teams and social services play in the delivery of e2e?

Different local support agencies play a valuable role in the provision of a holistic service for young people. These agencies may work with young people engaged on e2e by offering them the support they need. In other instances, learning providers may refer young people to local support agencies to deal with particular issues such as drug or alcohol dependency, sexual health issues or child abuse.

The provision of aftercare services within e2e after you have completed your programme ensures smoother transition and onward progression.

Modern Apprenticeships (MAs)

What is a Modern Apprenticeship?

A modern apprenticeship is where a number of essential learning elements have been brought together to create an integrated learning framework. They offer learners a whole package of learning that has been designed to meet the needs of a particular industry or sector of the economy.

There are over 150 types of Modern Apprenticeship in over 80 industries, including engineering, retail, information technology, floristry, accounting and financial services. This provides a great variety of occupations in which to work and train.

So, if you decide to follow a modern apprenticeship, you will develop the knowledge and skills needed to work in a particular industry.

How do I get started on a Modern Apprenticeship?

There are several ways to become an apprentice. You can apply for an MA online at www.apprenticeships.org.uk, or through the Connexions Service who will know which local employers provide Modern Apprenticeships. Or you may simply respond to an advertisement, as employers do advertise Modern Apprenticeships through their normal recruitment procedures. You should contact the Connexions Service anyway if you are not already in touch. They will give you the guidance you need.

What will I learn on a Modern Apprenticeship?

Because Modern Apprenticeships are learning frameworks you would:

- develop your personal and social skills
- develop the knowledge and skills you need to do the job – the technical know-how
- develop other skills that help people to be successful in the workplace

such as communication skills, numeracy, information technology, working with others, and problem solving

- learn how to apply what you have learned in the work place – your occupational competence.

If I learn this much, what qualification will I get?

As you progress through the Modern Apprenticeship programme you will become qualified in a number of areas and you will collect a number of certificates to demonstrate this. For example, as you develop your knowledge and skills you will collect a number of technical certificates. As you develop other skills that can be used in the workplace you will collect a number of Key Skills certificates. Once you have proved that you can apply the knowledge and skills required for the job you will be awarded with the appropriate NVQ certificate. Then to top it all off and once all these certificates have been awarded, you can claim your Modern Apprenticeship certificate. This is like a final diploma that confirms you have completed all the requirements of the learning framework. In addition, you may also get a reference from your employer.

What are Technical Certificates?

Technical Certificates are qualifications that recognise that you have learned the specific occupational knowledge required to do a job. You will gain this knowledge through off-the-job training where you would be taught in a classroom, or you might follow a distance-learning course through the Internet. In order to be awarded a Technical Certificate you will need to take an external assessment where you could be required to:

- complete a case study, project or assignment that is externally marked
- take a multiple choice question paper
- take a written examination
- attend a 'viva' where you could be asked to make a presentation and answer interview questions.

Some Technical Certificates are new and have been developed to meet the needs of a particular sector. This is because qualifications that assessed essential knowledge did not exist previously. In other cases existing qualifications such as a BTEC National Diploma or a City and Guilds vocational certificate have been included in many Modern Apprenticeship frameworks to meet the technical certificate requirements.

What are Key Skills?

Key skills are a range of essential generic skills that you will need in your working and personal life. You will be able to apply these skills as you continue to learn, work and run your personal life. In an ever-changing society you will have to communicate, understand numbers and use information technology. These have become essential key skills if you are to compete effectively in the labour market.

The key skill qualifications of Communication and Application of Numbers at level 2 are now a mandatory requirement in all Advanced Modern Apprenticeship frameworks. But you would be well advised to go past this minimum requirement and do these key skills at level three. You may even want to do other key skills in IT, improving your own learning and performance, problem solving and working with others at different levels. It is up to you to take advantage of all the key skills on offer.

What is a National Vocational Qualification (NVQ)?

NVQs assess occupational competence, which is your ability to apply all your knowledge and skills in the workplace to get jobs done on time and to specification. In order to prove that you are occupationally competent you will be assessed in the workplace completing real work activities. The idea of an NVQ is to see if you can cope with the unplanned and unexpected, respond to additional demands, requests, pressures and problems that arise in jobs all the time and every day. Once you have proved that you have met the occupational standards contained in the NVQ specification you will be awarded the appropriate NVQ certificate.

Where and how will learning take place?

Learning is delivered through a mixture of off-the-job and on-the-job learning.

The amount of off-the-job training you will be expected to do on a Modern apprenticeship will vary according to what Technical Certificates have been included in the framework. But it is fair to say that you will be required to spend time with a learning provider studying for your Technical Certificates and learning more about what is required in the key skills.

When you are out in the workplace you will be able to practise what you have learned so that you develop the knowledge you need to do the job and hone the essential skills required for the job.

What is the difference between a FMA and an AMA?

There are two different levels of Modern Apprenticeship, which are as follows:

- **Foundation Modern Apprenticeship (FMA)**

On a Foundation Modern Apprenticeship you'll have a job and a wage. If this is not possible you will go on a work placement and be given a weekly training allowance of £40. An FMA takes at least 18 months to complete and leads to the award of an NVQ at level 2, technical certificates and key skills certificates. The work is mainly practical: you'll develop technical skills and gain valuable work experience. There is also the opportunity to progress to an Advanced Modern Apprenticeship.

- **Advanced Modern Apprenticeship (AMA)**

On an Advanced Modern Apprenticeship, you'll be in full-time employment with an appropriate wage. This means that you will enjoy employed status. You should be aiming for a technical, supervisory or junior management role. The training, which usually lasts at least 24 months, leads to the award of an NVQ at level 3, technical certificates and key skills certificates. For many, an AMA is a stepping-stone to university where people might start a Foundation Degree.

Who designs the frameworks?

Sector Skills Councils set out what is appropriate for their particular sector. This ensures that the skills you learn are useful to the industry you wish to work in. They decide

- what entry requirements you will need to get on the programme
- what technical certificates to include in the programme
- what level of key skills is required in the programme
- what NVQ to include in the programme
- how long the programme should last.

Are you eligible to join a Modern Apprenticeship?

There are no set entry requirements to do a Modern Apprenticeship. You just need to be living in England, aged 16-24 and not taking part in full-time education.

But the Sector Skills Councils may ask for certain GCSE passes. This is because they want you to be successful and they recognise that an AMA can be really demanding. Many frameworks require well-developed study skills. However, if you show enthusiasm for the sector and a willingness to learn, some employers and learning providers will let you onto the programme. If this happens they will often ask you to do additional work to give you the skills you need to be successful. For example, you may be given additional help with your basic skills if they are poor. Ultimately, the selection of a Modern Apprentice rests with the employer to ensure they get the person that they feel is right for their business.

It is unusual for people to be taken on a Modern Apprenticeship if they are 19 years of age or older. The local learning and skills councils can make exceptions if they feel that the person stands to benefit a great deal from the programme. People of 19 are not considered to be a priority to the LSC in terms of recruitment to Modern Apprenticeship programmes.

However, the kind of skills and attributes employers are looking for in a potential modern apprentice are the

- motivation to succeed in the sector of your choice
- willingness to learn and apply that learning in the workplace
- ability to demonstrate that you have the potential to complete the qualifications which are part of the programme
- willingness to communicate with a range of people
- willingness to undergo a police check (you would need to do this to enter employment in sectors such as childcare)

Modern Apprenticeships should be about raising standards so that graduates from these programmes can be successful in the workplace.

How much will you be paid?

You're guaranteed a basic wage or training allowance of at least £40 a week. But you could get more depending on your employer.

Do you get holidays?

You'll get at least 1.5 days' paid holiday for every month of your training. On top of that you'll get bank holidays.

Can you become a Modern Apprentice you are already in work?

It is possible to become a Modern Apprentice when you are already in a job. Your employer might ask you if you want to be an apprentice because they have decided to invest in your future. Or you could approach your employer and ask if they want to make you a Modern Apprentice. In either event you can always seek advice from your local Connexions Service.

Leaving an Apprenticeship before completion

If you want to leave, or your job gets made redundant or your relationship with your employer breaks down, the normal rules as stated in your employer's terms and conditions of employment will apply. But it is your learning provider's duty to find you an alternative Modern Apprenticeship programme.[2]

What happens at the end of a Modern Apprenticeship?

The qualifications gained on an AMA can help you to go on to higher education if you want to or you can stay with your employer and develop your career. If you have completed an FMA you can go on and do an AMA. You could go and work for another employer. You could even become self-employed. Or you could go to a FE College and take some higher qualifications. The choice is yours. But the Modern Apprenticeship will open up a large range of opportunities for you.

Summary

What follows is a summary of your options:

Staying in the sixth form

For many, the good thing about school sixth form is that you can continue learning in familiar surroundings and with teachers you already know. You can move to another sixth form in another school if you want to. Most sixth formers take AS subjects in the first year and then make a choice on what subjects to take at A level in their second year. But many schools now offer a range of other courses, such as VCEs, so ask what's available. What's on offer will depend partly on how many people are in the sixth form and if the school has arrangements with other local schools or colleges to give you a wider choice

Going to a sixth-form college

You could continue your studies in a sixth-form college where you are likely to be offered a large range of GCEs and VCEs. The social life might not be bad either.

Going to FE

Further education colleges vary a lot; depending on what else is on offer locally. If most local schools have sixth forms, or there are local sixth-form colleges, the FE College may specialise in vocational courses that closely link to the needs of commerce and industry. Successful completion of these courses can lead to university entry.

In other areas, the FE College is the only – or the main – option after 16, and will also offer everything you could get in a school sixth form or sixth-form college. All FE colleges will have part-time and adult students, and may have more than one site. In some cases, FE colleges have separate 'sixth form centres'. You can do GCEs and VCEs as well as other more traditional vocational subjects.

Joining an Entry to Employment (e2e) programme

If you're not quite sure what you want to do, or are trying to overcome a barrier in your personal life that would prevent you from getting a job, you should think about Entry to Employment (e2e). This will give you the confidence and skills you need to enter the workplace. Each e2e programme is tailored to suit you and you'll cover a range of activities that will help to prepare you for work. You may go on to a work placement and receive vocational training or you may be working as part of a small group and get one-to-one attention to improve your skills and help you overcome any barriers. You'll also get paid a weekly training allowance and expenses.

Following a Modern Apprenticeship Programme

If you are keen to get your teeth into a job straightaway, you may want to consider a Modern Apprenticeship, where you can earn and learn. As a modern apprentice you will learn on and off the job, build up your knowledge and skills, gain qualifications and earn money. Modern Apprenticeships are designed to equip you with the skills and experience you need to climb your chosen career ladder.

A Modern Apprenticeship does not last for a fixed length of time – it ends when all necessary elements have been completed and the employer's requirements are satisfied. However, they tend to last for between a minimum of 18 months and three years.

On a Foundation Modern Apprenticeship, you'll have a job and be paid a wage, or you will be on a work placement with a weekly training allowance.

On an Advanced Modern Apprenticeship, you'll be in full-time employment with an appropriate wage for the job you are doing, aiming for a technical, supervisory or junior management role.

Entering the workplace

You might be keen to get out there and earn money. However don't forget your long-term future in your hurry to earn cash now. It's really important to a get a job with training – planned training, that leads to nationally recognised qualifications. This is because jobs for people with low skills and no qualifications are disappearing; you will also earn less money in the long run.

But if you do take this option, remember you have the right to time off for study or training.

Endnotes

[1] The costs of courses run by school sixth forms, sixth-form colleges, different FE Colleges and work-based learning providers are paid for by the Learning and Skills Council.

[2] Foundation and Advanced Modern Apprenticeships: guidance on the development of frameworks. Version 5. April 2002. DfES/ LSC)

5 Financial support for young people in particular circumstances

Benefits for young people with a disability or a long-term health problem

If you have a health problem or disability, you may be entitled to certain benefits. Unlike Jobseeker's Allowance, there are no restrictions on entitlement because of your age or because you are in care or a care leaver.

Some of the benefits can still be paid even if you are in work, education or training.

Who can claim?

If you are aged 16 or older, you can claim these benefits in your own right. If a parent or carer has been receiving disability benefits for you as your 'appointee', you can ask for the appointeeship to be revoked (or the appointee can resign). You then receive the benefits in your own right, even if your disability means that you have difficulty coping with or understanding the benefits system.

Appointees must spend the benefits on behalf of the person they receive them for.[1]

Disability Living Allowance (DLA)

DLA is a benefit which can be paid if you need extra care or support or you have difficulty getting around. It is not based on your income or savings. It is tax-free and can be paid on top of other benefits – indeed, it can even increase some benefits such as Income Support. There is no list of which illnesses or disabilities will qualify and it's not just those people who have very apparent disabilities who qualify. People with moderate learning disabilities, substance misuse problems, severe behavioural problems and mental health difficulties as well as more serious disabilities and health problems can qualify.

You must be able to show that you have met the rules for DLA for at least three months (unless you have a terminal illness).

DLA can be paid even if you don't have a carer and whether you live with parents or on your own.

There are two parts (components) to DLA – a care component and a mobility component and there are three rates of the care component and two of the mobility component. It is possible to qualify for either component or one component on its own, but you can only receive one of the rates.

Who qualifies?

The care component

The rate you qualify for depends on the amount of help you need and whether or not you need help during either day or night or both day and night. For all rates, you don't need to show that you receive the help you need, just show that the help is 'reasonably required'.

The low rate [2]

You must need help with 'bodily functions' (i.e. all the things that your body does) at least once a day and for at least a 'significant' time (either in one single period or more than one). You can also qualify if you are aged at least 16 and are unable to prepare and cook a main meal. You may qualify if you need reminding to take medication each day or supervision to prevent self-harm or if you need a bit of help with a daily task.

The middle rate [3]

You must need frequent help with bodily functions during each day or you must need someone available almost all the time during the day in case there's a possibility that you would get into danger or cause danger to others

or

during the night you need 'frequent or prolonged' help with bodily functions or you need someone to be awake for a long time or at 'frequent intervals' to look in on you during the night.

The high rate [4]

If you satisfy both one of the day and one of the night conditions, or you have a terminal illness, you qualify for the higher rate.

The mobility component

Again, the rate you get depends on how much difficulty you have getting around. Your ability to walk is assessed taking account of any equipment you use such as a stick or artificial limb.

The lower rate [5]

You qualify for the lower rate if you need someone to guide or supervise you most of the time in places that you are not familiar with. Your disability could be physical or mental.

The higher rate [6]

There are six different ways to qualify for the higher rate. Your difficulty walking must have a physical origin.

- You are unable to walk, or
- You are virtually unable to walk because of a combination of factors such as how far you can walk, how fast, how long you can walk for, the

way you walk and whether or not you can walk without pain or severe discomfort, or

- The exertion of walking would endanger your health (for example because of cardiac or respiratory problems), or
- You have no legs or feet, or
- You are both deaf and blind, or
- You are also entitled to the higher rate care component and you have a severe mental impairment which means your behaviour is both disruptive and dangerous.

To qualify for DLA, you must have satisfied the conditions of entitlement for at least three months and also be expected to satisfy them for another three months after you claim.[7]

How to claim

You can claim by getting a claim form from the DWP's Benefits Enquiry Line on 0800 882200. You can also complete a claim form online at www.dwp.gov.uk/eservice/. If you phone to make a claim, you will be sent a claim form which is date stamped and you then have six weeks to complete and return the whole form. This ensures that your claim is dated from the date of your phone call. An online claim will be dated from when you register. You may also claim by downloading a claim form from the DWP website or by picking up a claim form from a local advice agency. However, your claim will then be dated from the date the completed form is received by the DWP.

It is important to take time to complete the form and to fully explain your needs and how much help you need. Use the additional spaces on the form to show how and why you need help each day and the type of help you need. Also describe how your disability or health problem affects you and why this means that you need help from others. There is also space on the form for a carer and someone who knows you in a professional capacity to add information – it is best to ask someone who knows your needs well rather than someone who you think has the most qualifications. Your doctor should counter-sign to confirm your medical condition.

It is also a good idea to keep a diary for a typical day showing what help you need hour by hour. Enclose this with the claim form as evidence.

Awards of DLA are made for any period from six months to an indefinite period. Before awarding the higher rate mobility component, or also if the DWP think that more information is needed, you may be asked to undergo an examination by a doctor contracted to work for them. You can have someone with you during this examination to help you put over your case. You may also be asked to undergo a medical examination if the DWP decide to look at your claim again or if they feel that your health has changed.

If you are unhappy with the amount you have been awarded (or you have been turned down altogether), you can appeal and also ask them to look at the decision again. You must normally do this within one month of being sent the decision. Seek independent advice if this applies to you.

If you live in certain types of accommodation [8]

If you stay in accommodation which is funded in whole or part by the NHS or by Social Services – (but only if this is paid for by them under Part III National Assistance Act 1948 or Part IV Social Work (Scotland) Act 1968 or education legislation or similar legislation) your DLA care component should be suspended after 28 days. This could apply if you live in a children's home, a residential school, or a residential care home. Shorter periods than this which are separated by less than another 28 days can be added together to reach the 28 day suspension time limit. If you are receiving free in-patient NHS treatment, your mobility component is also suspended.

Accommodation which is not affected by this rule includes:

- Foster-parent accommodation ;
- Respite care with a family who are paid by Social Services/Social Work Department to look after you;
- Accommodation where you pay rent;
- Housing for homeless people.

It is important to tell the DWP if you move into any of the types of accommodation which affect your benefits and to also tell them as soon as you know you will leave. If you live in accommodation where you can't normally receive DLA, you can still receive it for any time spent away – for example, weekends with parents.

Incapacity Benefit

People who claim after October 2008 will be affected by Employment Support Allowance which replaces new claims for IB after that date.

Incapacity Benefit (IB) is a benefit for people aged 16 or older who are unable to work because of physical or mental ill health or disability. If you are employed and are paying National Insurance Contributions, you will qualify for Statutory Sick Pay for up to 28 weeks. This is paid by your employer. After 28 weeks, if you are still unable to work, you will qualify for Incapacity Benefit.

Normally you must have paid sufficient National Insurance Contributions in order to qualify for IB. However young people can qualify without having enough National Insurance Contributions.[9]

If you receive Incapacity Benefit, it will mean that your parents/carers can no longer claim any benefits or tax credits for you. This may mean that the family income as a whole will be less, so it is important to seek advice about your family's finances before making a claim for Incapacity Benefit.

IB is paid at one of three weekly three rates:

- Lower short term rate
- Higher short term rate, or
- Long term rate.

In addition, people whose incapacity for work starts before they reach the age of 35 also receive an age-related addition of £17.10 a week on top of the long term rate.

People with adult dependant(s) who have low enough earnings may also receive a dependant's addition for them.

If you are under 20 when your incapacity for work started, to qualify without enough National Insurance Contributions you must:

- have been incapable of work for at least 196 consecutive days (i.e. 28 weeks); and
- if you are under 19, not be in full-time education. This is defined as being 21 hours or more a week of supervised study, but it does not include any education or training which is not suitable for people without a disability.[10]

There are also rules to allow those aged between 20 and 25 to make a new claim and qualify without enough National Insurance Contributions (these are not covered in this book).

IB cannot be paid for the first three days of incapacity of work and the 28 weeks of incapacity for work must be a continuous period with no breaks to go into work or training.

Claims

You should claim as soon as you think you may be incapable of work. If you have been incapable of work before the age of 16, provided that you claim within three months of your 16th birthday, you will not have to wait the full 28 weeks to qualify. It is also possible for your claim to be backdated up to three months. It is also usually best to claim Income Support at the same time as you claim IB, just in case you don't get IB.

What is incapacity for work?

To be accepted as incapable of work for Incapacity Benefit, you must:

- be incapable of following your own occupation for up to 28 weeks and supply medical certificates ('sick notes') . For the first seven days you provide a 'self-certificate' and then you will need to supply medical certificates from your doctor. If you have not been employed for at least 16 hours a week for at least 8 out of the last 21 weeks, you will need to pass the Personal Capability Assessment (PCA). You will also have to pass the PCA straight away if you have not been in work for at least 16 hours a week for 8 or more weeks [11]

- after 28 weeks, you must pass the PCA. The PCA is a test looking at various physical and mental abilities. You will be asked to complete a questionnaire (IB 50) or to attend a medical examination by a doctor working for the DWP who will carry out the PCA. This leads to you being given a number of points, based on how ill or disabled you are. If you do not score enough points, the DWP will then decide whether or not you qualify for IB (usually your claim will be refused).[12]

Most people who are given too low a score on the PCA succeed in increasing their score when they appeal.

The PCA considers a range of physical abilities (for example, walking, manual dexterity, speech and reaching) and mental abilities (for example, completing tasks, daily living, coping with pressure and interacting with people) and you receive a score depending on the extent of your abilities. It is important to highlight the full extent of your difficulties and to seek independent help if you are at all unsure.

You must score at least 15 points under the physical abilities list or 10 points under the mental abilities list. Or if you score between 6 and 9 on the mental abilities list, these are rounded up to 9 and you can add these to any physical ability scores to reach 15.[13]

You can be exempted from the PCA if you are deemed to be incapable of work. This includes people who are:

- in hospital
- pregnant and there is a risk to your or the baby's health
- within six weeks before or 14 days after giving birth
- classed as a 'welfare to work beneficiary' by the DWP and reclaiming IB within 52 weeks of previously receiving it
- suspected of carrying an infectious or contagious disease
- receiving certain medical treatments: plasmapheresis, parental chemotherapy, radiotherapy, weekly renal dialysis or total parenteral nutrition treatment.

You can also be exempted from the PCA if you:

- are registered as blind;
- receive the highest rate DLA care component;
- have a severe learning disability which severely impairs intelligence and social functioning;
- have a severe mental illness which severely and adversely affects your mood or behaviour and severely limits your ability to function socially or your awareness of what is happening around you;
- are terminally ill;
- suffer from a specific serious medical condition including: inflammatory arthritis, certain severe neurological or muscle wasting conditions, paralysis of one side of your body, severe heart problems, severe immune deficiency with other problems or the effects of a stroke or head injury or
- receive disablement benefit because of a work-related injury or disease and have been assessed as being at least 80% disabled.[14]

Even if you are capable of work, you should be treated as being incapable of work if there would be a substantial risk to the mental or physical health of any person if you were found capable of work.[15]

More than one period of incapacity for work

Normally you will not be entitled to IB for the first three days of sickness but if you are incapable of work at least twice within any eight weeks, the DWP ignore any subsequent first three days. However, you must still serve the initial 28 weeks' period of incapacity for work. If you are receiving IB after 196 days' incapacity for work, and you stop receiving it because you start work or training, it is possible to reclaim IB within 104 weeks without having to wait another 28 weeks.[16]

Working while receiving Incapacity Benefit [17]

It is possible to work for less than 16 hours a week and to continue to receive IB in certain situations so long as you work less than 16 hours and earn less than £86.00 a week (this rate is expected to increase slightly from October 2007). This is known as 'Permitted Work'. For more on this go to www.jobcentreplus.gov.uk .

There is no limitation on voluntary work done for your expenses.

Incapable of work if employed

Most employees qualify for Statutory Sick Pay rather than Incapacity Benefit if they are employed (even if they only work part-time) and they are incapable of work.

People on work-based training

Trainees who are employed will normally qualify for Statutory Sick Pay. Those who are not employees will either qualify for Incapacity Benefit or for Income Support on the ground of incapacity for work (see page 34).

Incapacity Benefit and Income Support (IS)

Most young people who qualify for the long-term rate of IB (paid after a year's incapacity for work) will have an income which puts them above IS level, unless they also qualify for additional premiums in their IS – such as the severe disability or enhanced disability premium, which may be awarded if you get DLA Care. It is important to check this point.

If you are waiting to complete the 28 week period of incapacity for work to qualify for IB, you may qualify for IS. And if you have a disability or ill-health but don't qualify for IB (for example, if you are in full-time education or are not treated as Incapable of Work), you may qualify for Income Support even if you live with your parents.

It is possible to receive both Disability Living Allowance and IB and you should claim both if you think you qualify – it may increase entitlement to means-tested benefits because you may qualify for additional 'premiums'.

If you make a claim for IB or IS and you are under 18, you don't have to attend a work or learning focused interview with either Jobcentre Plus or Connexions/Careers Service.

Sickness while claiming Jobseeker's Allowance

You should notify the Jobcentre as soon as you are sick because you can continue to claim JSA for up to two weeks if you are sick.[18] If you are unable to attend the Jobcentre to sign on because of sickness, you should also tell them immediately in order to prevent your payments being disrupted. They should then send you a form so that you can notify them about your sickness – you must complete and return this to safeguard your benefit. You can continue receiving JSA while sick for up to two fortnightly periods in every 12 months that you receive JSA.

If you are sick for more than two weeks, or if your sickness is expected to last for more than two weeks, you will have to make a claim for Income Support, or if you have enough National Insurance Contributions, for short-term lower-rate IB.

If you fail to sign on on the right day, you have to sign a written declaration within a further five working days that you had 'good cause' for not signing on on your normal day. This might include a few days' sickness. Your JSA claim should not be stopped (but payment of benefit will be delayed).[19]

Accidents or diseases which are related to work or training

If you have an accident, or contract a 'prescribed disease' (PD), in the course of your work or work-based learning and as a result you are still suffering some disability 15 weeks later, you may qualify for Industrial Injuries Disablement Benefit (IIDB).

(The full list of PDs is available in the CPAG Welfare Benefits and Tax Credits Handbook, and the Disability Rights Handbook. There is some information in DWP leaflet No SD 6 – "Ill or Disabled because of a disease or deafness caused by work?" And at www.jobcentreplus.gov.uk)

Employed learners can make a claim for IIDB through Jobcentre Plus.

Unwaged learners/trainees can make a claim to IIDB through the Analogous Industrial Injuries Scheme at the Department for Work and Pensions – call 01977 464094.

The Analogous Industrial Injuries Scheme (AIIS) is a discretionary scheme, which uses the same guidance, the same doctors and pays benefits at the same rates as Jobcentre Plus. It covers non-employed learners on work-based learning that is funded by the LSC, and its equivalent organisations in Scotland and Wales, or by the Department for Work and Pensions (DWP). It does not cover work experience placements, or any non-employed status learning that might be arranged privately, through schools, or through Further Education Colleges.

How to claim

If you have an accident or contract a prescribed disease as a result of your work you should inform your employer and learning provider as soon as possible. Your learning provider must then send a report to the Learning and Skills Council (LSC).

If you do not have employed status, the LSC will send this report to the AIIS team. The AIIS team will write to you with information about the scheme and invite you to start the claims process.

If you have employed status, it is up to you to start the claims process by contacting your local Jobcentre Plus office, or you can download a form from the Jobcentre Plus website.

Making a claim to Disablement Benefit does not stop you taking legal action against your employer or training provider. However, compensation awarded by the court may be reduced by the amount of benefits you receive. DWP booklet GL27, Compensation and social security benefits, has more details.

The AIIS is at: Analogous Industrial Injuries Scheme, Bridge House, 28 Wheldon Road, Castleford WF10 2JG. Phone: 01977 464094

What happens next

A Decision Maker (DM) from within Jobcentre Plus or from the AIIS team, depending on your status, will decide if your accident counts as an industrial accident and you will be sent a copy of the decision. If your accident is accepted you can make a claim for benefit.

If you have contracted a 'prescribed disease' a decision will not normally be given until you have attended a medical examination.

If the doctor's assessment of your disability is at least 14%, IIDB is paid at a rate determined by the extent of your disability. You don't need to show that you are permanently disabled as awards can range from a few months to a lifetime. IIDB can be paid 15 weeks after the date of an accident, or the date a prescribed disease (PD) was contracted (Even if you have continued with your training during this time, you can still apply for IIDB.) IIDB does not depend on National Insurance contributions.

If you are awarded IIDB at 100% and need daily care and attention, you may be entitled to payment of Constant Attendance Allowance.

If you have received a means-tested benefit e.g. Income Support (IS) or income-based Job Seeker's Allowance (JSA) since your accident, you may not be entitled to receive some or any arrears of disablement benefits. IIDB counts as income for income-based benefits. Therefore if you are getting a means-tested benefit now, this may be reduced by the amount of IIDB payable. Payment of IIDB is not affected by Incapacity Benefit, Statutory Sick Pay, Training Allowance or earnings – this means it can be a useful welfare to work benefit.

Appeals

To appeal against a DM's decision you should follow the advice on the decision letter. Take note of any time limits for making an appeal. You may be asked to attend a further medical examination to enable a fair decision to be made on your claim.

Benefits for young people from abroad and those who are subject to immigration control

Information in this book about benefits assumes that you will not have problems claiming because of your residence or immigration status or because you have recently arrived in the UK.

People from abroad often face restrictions on their right to receive benefits and tax credits. It is a complex area and one where it is easy to make mistakes, so specialist independent help is essential because this chapter is just a general introduction to some of the issues involved.

There are links between the Home Office and the Department for Work and Pensions. If your stay in the UK is subject to immigration control, you should not even inquire about your benefit entitlement unless you have sought skilled, independent advice and help. Even an enquiry may result in a criminal offence being committed and/or removal from the UK or refusal of permission to enter or remain in the UK in the future.

Further information is available in the Newcomer's Handbook published by *Inclusion* and also the Child Poverty Action Group's Welfare Benefits and Tax Credits Handbook and the Migration and Social Security Handbook.

Financial support for young people who are looked after by local authorities or who have left care

If you are in local authority care (known as 'looked after') or if you have been looked after and are under 18, you may be barred from claiming some benefits. But you may be entitled to receive extra help and support from the local authority which was legally responsible for you or even from the council where you live.

The part of the local authority which is responsible for looked-after children and young people and care leavers is the Social Services Department (in Scotland, the Social Work Department). This department may also be known as 'Children's Service' or 'Children and Families Service'.

The Children (Leaving Care) Act 2000

This law came into force in England and Wales in October 2001. Similar law came into force in Scotland in April 2004. The law applies to most but not all young people who are in or who have just left local authority care. Your social worker will be able to tell you if it applies to you.

This legislation amended the Children Act 1989, but only applies to young people who left care after October 2001. The Children (Scotland)

Act 1995 has also been amended along the same lines from April 2004. A young person who left the care of a Scottish local authority before 1st April 2004 is not included.

You are covered by this legislation in England and Wales if you are an 'eligible', 'relevant' or 'former relevant' young person. There are also 'qualifying' young people.

In Scotland there are categories of young people who are classed as a 'compulsorily supported person', 'currently looked after person' or 'discretionarily supported person'.[20]

If you are looked after by a local authority for at least 13 weeks after your 14th birthday, including a period when you are aged 16, (in Scotland within three months of becoming compulsorily supported or within three months of when someone who may be supported asks for help) the local authority should tell you which category you fall into.[21]

If you are classed as what the law calls a relevant or eligible young person (or the equivalent in Scotland), the local authority must carry out an assessment of your current and future needs within three months of your turning 16. They will then prepare a 'pathway plan' explaining how your needs will be met.[22] The assessment should consider your training, education and employment needs, your need for financial support, accommodation and other matters.[23]

The Pathway Plan explains the support you will receive for leaving care. It also states who your leaving care personal adviser is. The Pathway Plan must be reviewed at least every six months or sooner if you ask for it to be reviewed or your personal adviser feels it should be. If you are not happy with the Pathway Plan, not only can you ask for it to be reviewed, but also you can make a formal complaint.

Eligible young people

You are 'eligible' if you are 16 or 17, are currently looked after by a local authority and you have also been looked after by a local authority for at least 13 weeks since the age of 14. The 13 weeks don't have to be continuous, but regular planned, short periods in care where you returned to live with your parents afterwards (for example because you have a disability and go into respite care) do not count towards the 13 weeks.

Relevant young people

You are 'relevant' if you are 16 or 17 and have been looked after by a local authority for at least 13 weeks since you were 14 but you are no longer looked after. You are also 'relevant' if you would have been a relevant young person but when you turned 16 you were in custody or hospital.

Former relevant young people (No equivalent in Scotland)

You are classed as a 'former relevant' young person if you were either a relevant or eligible young person and you are now aged 18, 19 or 20.

Qualifying young person

A 'qualifying' young person (or a 'compulsorily supported person' in Scotland) is someone under 18 who has been in care at the age of 16 but for less than 13 weeks since the age of 14, even if they have since left care.

A discretionarily supported person (Scotland)

A discretionarily supported young person is one aged 19 or 20, who has been looked after at any time since the age of 16, but who is not a compulsorily supported person.

Child in need (also in Scotland)

You may be helped with accommodation, assistance in cash and other help and support if you are a 'child in need' because of special needs, poverty, poor housing, ill-health or family or other difficulties, and the help is designed to prevent you having to be looked after.[24] This is known as a Section 17 payment and support. All payments under this legislation are ignored as income for benefits, but may be taken into account if they are meeting a need which you claim a Social Fund crisis loan for or you are claiming JSA on the grounds of severe hardship.

A local authority is not allowed to restrict its discretion about whom or how it will help under S 17 Children Act (S 22 Children (Scotland) Act 1995) by having blanket rules.[25] Acting unreasonably or failing to act reasonably under S 17 can leave a local authority open to legal challenge.[26]

A child in need, getting occasional help under S 17 (S 22 in Scotland), has no restrictions on the benefits they can claim, other than those that apply to all 16-17 year olds.

However, if you receive help with accommodation or money on an ongoing basis under S 17/22, Jobcentre Plus staff might try to argue that you are actually an eligible, relevant or former relevant young person and refuse you benefits.[27] This shouldn't happen if the support given under S 17/22 for accommodation was made after November 7th. 2002. (From 7.11.02 the law was amended so that a child who is 'looked after' does not include someone provided with accommodation under Section 17/22).

The Hillingdon court case also means that if you have been supported after the age of sixteen under S17/22 and provided with accommodation and lots of support and help, the local authority may have obligations to support you financially and in the same way as care leavers are supported. However, you may need legal advice in order to ensure that Social Services/Social Work Department provides support in these circumstances.

DWP guidance issued in 2003[28] isn't very clear on that point and you might find that you have restricted benefit entitlement. At the time of writing, this aspect of the law is not settled and it would be worth challenging negative decisions.

Benefits for eligible, relevant and qualifying young people

If you are an eligible or relevant young person (or you are a compulsorily supported young person or are currently looked after in Scotland), you can't receive Housing Benefit or Jobseeker's Allowance at all.[29] You can only receive Income Support if you are:

- a lone parent,

- a single foster parent,
- incapable of work or have appealed against a decision that you are not incapable of work,
- a disabled worker whose earning power is 75% or less or you work while living in a care home,
- a disabled or deaf student in higher education,
- a student in education up to and including A level standard who is either a lone parent, or disabled (getting any rate of DLA).

These restrictions only apply until you are 18. If you go back home to live with parents or other adults, you will still be barred from claiming JSA for six months, or until you reach 18, whichever comes first. You could get IS during that time though if you are in any of the above categories.[30]

If you are a relevant or eligible young person (and the equivalent in Scotland) you are able to claim all other benefits – for example, Disability Living Allowance, Carer's Allowance, Incapacity Benefit and Child Benefit if you meet the rules for those benefits. But even if you can receive Income Support, you are still barred from claiming Housing Benefit until you are 18.

If you are a qualifying young person there are no restrictions on the benefits you can receive provided that you meet the rules of entitlement, including the rules of entitlement for 16 and 17 year olds to receive Jobseeker's Allowance (see page 40).

There is sometimes confusion about benefits when you reach 18 and stay living with your former foster carers. At that point, you can claim JSA in your own right without restriction, if you haven't been eligible to Income Support as a 16/17 year old already. You can also then claim housing benefit if your ex-foster carers charge you rent.

Rights to financial support from Social Services (Social Work Department in Scotland)

If you are an eligible, relevant and former relevant young person (or in Scotland you are looked after, were looked after for at least 13 weeks since the age of 14 or are a Compulsorily Supported Person) you have rights to financial and other support from the local authority which last looked after you. Qualifying young people (and in Scotland Discretionarily Supported People) can also be helped on a discretionary basis.

The Pathway Plan if you are a relevant, eligible or former relevant young person must set out the support you need and what you can expect to receive. Specifically it must contain information about the following:[31]

- Personal support accommodation
- Education or training
- Employment or other activity or occupation
- Family and social relationships
- Practical and other skills for independent living
- Financial support
- Health needs
- Contingency plans if the pathway plan breaks down.

Pathway Plans should build on the existing Education Plans and intentions which you have and they must show how Social Services will help you to stay in or move into education, training or employment.

For relevant and eligible young people, there must be transparent criteria for financial support. Social Services must keep a list of what it would normally provide financial help for and how they will treat any income you may have.[32]

Things which must be considered as a priority for financial support are:

- travel costs for e.g. education,
- educational materials/special equipment,
- other educational costs,
- costs associated with special needs (such as a disability or pregnancy),
- the costs of childcare,
- clothing,

- contact with family or other significant relationships,
- cultural/religious needs,
- counselling or therapeutic needs, and
- hobbies/holidays.

Your rights to financial support must be fully explained to you. This list is not a complete list of what can be provided, but there are no set amounts which Social Services should provide because the level of support is expected to reflect a young person's needs. Social Services may decide to apply sanctions (such as loss of privileges) but not such that you don't have enough to live on. Either with or without a sanction, you must receive at least the amount of help that you would have got through the benefit system.[33]

Some local councils are more generous than the benefit system would have been. They may pay 'rewards' if you attend training or find a job. But if you have an income from work or training, the council can still expect you to make some contribution to the cost of your care, rent, etc. However, they must take your circumstances into account and not apply blanket rules about how much you should contribute. If you are aged 16-17, looked-after and getting Income Support (or with an equivalent level of income) you cannot be asked to make a contribution to the cost of your care. If you are working or have an income from training, then you can be asked to contribute to the cost of your care but it has to be done properly, on a contribution notice. The council can't just pluck a figure out of the air!

If you are unhappy with the financial support you receive, you should ask to make a formal complaint and consider further action against Social Services. In Scotland this is known as 'an appeal'.[34]

If you are a former relevant young person under 21, Social Services have a duty to provide you with:

- a leaving care grant (this should be enough to set up home and may need to cover more than one attempt to set up home);
- sufficient financial support for you to finish education (even if this takes you beyond the age of 21), including travel, accommodation,

maintenance, tuition costs and vacation time accommodation;

- financial support to enable you to participate in or look for training or employment if you are under 24; and
- discretionary financial help if your welfare requires this.[35]

If you are a qualifying young person under the age of 21, Social Services must:[36]

- advise and befriend you;
- when necessary provide help in kind, or in exceptional circumstances in cash on a discretionary basis:
    - where it is connected with education, training or employment (which may continue beyond 21);
    - if other needs arise.

Social Services are also expected to give care leavers practical help and support to claim benefits.

Payments to care leavers which are made under the Children Act and equivalent Scottish and Northern Ireland legislation are all ignored as income and capital for all means-tested benefits and tax credits, unless you are involved in a trade dispute.[37]

If you are 18 or over, have ceased to be 'looked-after' and are still in non-advanced education, you may be able to receive Income Support up to your 20th birthday if you can show that you are 'estranged' from your natural parent(s). Social Services can provide extra help on top of Income Support and any Housing Benefit that you are due.

Housing Benefit

If you are under 22 and were looked after by a local authority after you were 16 for any length of time at all (i.e. for as little as one night), the Single Room Rent restriction doesn't apply. This is the rule which restricts your housing benefit in the private unregulated sector to the average rent for a single room in a shared house.[38] Because Housing Benefit claim forms do not usually ask about your care leaver status, it is important to check that the exemption has been granted and to also inform the local authority when a Housing Benefit claim is made.

However, you may still have a restriction applied under the Local Reference Rent rules.

You can't get Housing Benefit until you are aged 18 if you are in care or a care-leaver with restricted access to benefits, even if you are in one of the groups which qualify for Income Support.

But if you stay on with foster carers after 18 and they charge you rent, then you may receive Housing Benefit if you rent from them.[39]

Leaving Care Grant

When you leave care at 18, or sometime after if you don't need the money till then, the local authority may give you a grant to help to set you up in a place of your own. You might also qualify for a Social Fund grant in those circumstances too (see page 79).

Young people who need support with housing costs

Housing Benefit

What is Housing Benefit?

Housing Benefit (HB) helps you pay some or all of your rent. HB is administered by your local council.

Who can receive Housing Benefit?

You can receive HB if you are 16 or over and you have to pay rent (or other payments) to live somewhere – e.g. a hostel, flat, house or room. However, you won't be able to get HB for rent you pay to your parents or other close relatives if you live with them in the same address. Close relatives include brothers and sisters, but not aunts, uncles, cousins or grandparents. However, if the council think that you have set up a tenancy with that sort of relative, or anyone else for that matter, just to misuse housing benefit, they can refuse to pay it.

You must have less than £16,000 in savings or capital and you must also be on a low income – the amount of housing benefit you get depends on your income and family circumstances.

You do not need to receive Income Support (IS) or income-based Jobseeker's Allowance (ibJSA) in order to receive HB, but if you do (or if your income is at the same level as these benefits), you will qualify for the maximum amount of HB.

You can't get HB even if you pay rent if you are:

- subject to immigration control, do not have a right to reside in the UK or you are not habitually resident in the common travel area);
- a full-time student, unless you are in a group which qualifies for Income Support, or you are aged under 19 and not in higher education (University degree or higher), a lone parent, disabled, incapable of work for more than 28 weeks, or you are absent from your course with permission because of illness or caring responsibilities;[40]
- not renting on a commercial basis.[41]

If you are told you are excluded from getting HB for any reason then you should also get advice but you can always appeal and wait for a tribunal to tell if you are entitled (see below).

How much is Housing Benefit?

There are three main ways in which your HB award may be reduced. Firstly, the way in which rent is defined for HB purposes does not include all the services which your landlord provides for you. This means that some people who get HB (even those on IS/ibJSA) still have to pay a lot towards their landlord's rent charge. These are known as ineligible services and include:

- Water and sewage
- Heat and light (except in communal areas)
- Food
- Care and support.[42]

If you are charged for meals (for example, if you live in a hostel) there are also fixed deductions from your housing benefit depending on how many meals you get each day. There are also fixed deductions for heating and hot water charges etc. unless your landlord provides a different figure. There may also be deductions for support charges such as for cleaning your room. You can ask the local council to give you a written statement setting out what they have decided to pay for and then get advice on that or appeal.

Maximum eligible rent

HB may also be restricted because of where you live and because of your age.

Your HB can be reduced because of where you live or the type of accommodation you live in e.g. if it is too large for you. These reductions depend on who provides your accommodation and what age you are. If you rent your home from a local authority or housing association then most of these restrictions won't apply. However, if your accommodation is too large for you, e.g. a 2 bedroom flat for a single person, then your rent may be restricted to a 1 bedroom flat.

If you rent from a private landlord (not including a housing association) your rent will be restricted to an 'average' rent in the local area. A rent officer who is independent from the local authority sets the average rent. You or the local authority can ask the rent officer to reconsider the rent figure they have decided. Before you move into a property, you can ask the housing benefit office to ask the rent officer to carry out a pre-tenancy determination, which is an estimate of how much rent will be met by HB.

In some pilot areas, the council uses a 'Local Housing Allowance' instead of the rent officer. Fixed amounts are used for particular types of claimant instead of the rent that you are being charged. If your rent is more than the Allowance figure, you will have to find the shortfall. If your rent is less than the Allowance, you keep the difference. Local Housing Allowance goes nationwide from April 2008.

If you are aged less than 25 and have a private landlord, the rent officer will also calculate what it costs to rent a single room in a flat or house or a bedsit in the local area. The local council then has to compare the rents set by the rent officer for the local area and the 'single room rent'. Housing Benefit is restricted to the lower of those rents – the average rent or the single room rent.[43]

Some young people are not affected by the single room rent rule but are still affected by the average rent rule. You won't be affected by the single room rent rule if you have a child or a 'non-dependant' living with you, if you are severely disabled and get a severe disability premium with your HB or if you were accommodated by social services or you were in care and the court order still applied to you after you were 16. However, not all young people who were in care will be able to claim housing benefit – see rules about who can claim HB when you have been in care pages 138-9.

How Housing Benefit is calculated

People on IS or income-based JSA

If you get Income Support or income-based Jobseeker's Allowance you will have your maximum eligible rent paid for you. As we have seen your eligible rent is not the same as the amount you actually have to pay.

Other people who are on a low income

If you claim other benefits or if you are on a low income or training allowance then the local authority has to calculate your HB by calculating how much your income is above the fixed amounts and then deducting 65% of that 'excess' income from your eligible rent. The fixed amounts are called 'Applicable Amounts' and are made up of the 'personal allowances' and 'premiums' – set out in Appendix 2. If you think that you are entitled to more benefit than you are getting you should ask the local authority for an explanation of their calculation.

The 65% excess income is called a taper because of how it works: as your excess income goes up, your benefit goes down. You can have so much excess income that you do not qualify for any benefit.

Non-dependants

A non-dependant is someone who is aged 18 or over who is not part of your benefit claim. They must be permanently living with you but not on a commercial basis e.g. they are a lodger. Deductions are made from your HB for every non-dependant who lives with you (unless they are a couple). The law assumes they will contribute towards your rent whether or not they actually do so. The amount they are expected to contribute depends on how much they earn.[44] It is important to check that the right deduction is being made and to also tell the local authority if the non-dependant's earnings change.

No deduction should be made from your HB if you are registered as blind or you receive Disability Living Allowance care component (see page 123).[45]

If you are 18 or over and live with someone who gets housing benefit, or help from Income Support with their mortgage, you will be the one who has to make payment as a non-dependant to the person you live with to make up the cut in their benefit. This can be quite high – from £7.40 a week if you are 18 and getting JSA based on your NI contributions up to £47.75 a week if you earn more than £353 a week.

Occupying the home

You must live in the home for which you are claiming HB but you can live away from it for up to 13 weeks. You must intend to return to it and you must not sub-let it to someone else.[46] It doesn't matter what the reason is for living away from it. Other benefits have less generous rules if you are not living in your home so get advice.

It is possible to get HB paid on your property for up to 52 weeks whilst you are living somewhere else if it is for a specific reason, for example if you are in custody and you are on remand awaiting trial or you are in hospital.

If you move from one home to another

When you move from the home you were claiming HB on to another one you may be able to get HB on both homes for up to 4 weeks. To get this help you must have actually moved into the new home and your local authority must agree that you could not reasonably have avoided liability for rent on both your new home and your old home. For example, this may be because you have had to move because a training place or job has started unexpectedly. This rule only applies if you have actually moved into your new home and you have claimed housing benefit before you moved in. You also have to claim again after you move in.[47]

You will be able to get HB on more than one home if you move because of a fear that violence may occur to you in your home, or in the locality if this is due to a violent ex-partner or member of your family. In cases of violence you can get HB on both homes for up to 52 weeks – so long as you intend to return to your old home at some point and your local authority agrees it is reasonable to pay HB on both. However, if you do not intend to return home then you can only get HB for both for up to 4 weeks. There are some other more limited circumstances when it may be paid so get advice.

How to claim Housing Benefit

Housing Benefit claim forms are available from your local council and you can contact them for one. If you claim Income Support or income-based Jobseeker's Allowance you can complete a HB claim form as part of the claim pack. However, you must complete and return any claim forms the local authority send you after completing that one. Claimants often think that completing the claim form with their Income Support or Jobseeker's Allowance claim is enough. However, because of the way the claim system works you often have to complete the claim form twice. Recent government changes have attempted to abolish the need to complete the form twice but if the council sends you another claim form then you should complete it and return it as quickly as possible. You have four weeks from the time the council says it sent the form to you; even if this was some weeks before you got it.

If you can, try to get confirmation from the local council that they received it – such as a receipt if you take it to them. This is not always possible but you can make your own note of when you sent it or took it in or whom you spoke to.

If you have missed out on claiming HB, you can ask for your claim to be backdated 12 months from the date when you ask for backdating. Your claim must be backdated if you show that you have 'good cause' for claiming late.[48] This phrase is not defined in the legislation, but there is a lot of case law. Good cause for a late claim includes:

- sickness or disability which prevented you from claiming
- difficult personal circumstances which prevented you from claiming
- literacy and language difficulties
- being young and not being familiar with benefit rules
- a common misunderstanding which means that you have a 'mistaken belief reasonably held' (for example, a common misunderstanding is that you must be on IS/ibJSA to get HB).

You can appeal against a refusal to backdate a HB claim.

Evidence and information for your claim [49]

The council can ask you to provide evidence and information which is 'reasonably required' to assess your HB claim. If you don't provide this evidence and information, they must make a decision on your entitlement and not just shut down your claim. If the evidence does not exist or if obtaining it would involve cost or risk, it is not reasonable to require it and you should insist that your claim is processed with the evidence and information you can provide. The council should allow you one month or longer where reasonable to provide evidence and information.

Delays

The council has a legal duty to process your claim within 14 days of receiving all the information it needs.[50] Very few councils follow this deadline. If you are a private tenant (including a housing association tenant), the council also has a legal duty to make interim payments of HB 14 days after you made a claim unless they have asked you for evidence and information and you have not provided it without good cause.[51] Very few councils abide by the law and make these payments automatically, so you can ask for one to be made. The 'good cause' rule means that the council can only refuse if they have asked for the evidence and information and you don't have good reason for not supplying it.

Whom Housing Benefit is paid to

If you pay rent to the council then your HB is credited to your rent account. If you live in another type of accommodation such as renting from a private landlord or housing association then the rent may be paid directly to you but it can be paid to your landlord instead. It will be paid to your landlord if you ask for it to be paid to them or it is in your interests or you have at least eight weeks of rent arrears and the landlord asks for the payment. If you are in an area where local housing allowances are being tried out, your housing benefit will normally come straight to you.

Your HB claim lasts for a fixed period only. HB will tell you in the award letter how long it is for. It may only be for a few weeks but it can be up to a year. If you do not re-claim at the end of the award period you will no longer be entitled to HB.

If your circumstances change, you have a duty to notify your local authority in writing. If you do not, you will probably have to repay any overpayment.

Start of the payment period

The usual rule is that HB starts on the Monday after your date of claim for HB. Even if that date was a Monday, HB starts the following Monday. However, if your date of claim for HB is in the same benefit week as you moved into your home or first became liable for rent it should be paid from the Monday you moved in or became liable.

Overpayments[52]

Overpayments are amounts of HB which you were awarded but which you weren't entitled to for whatever reason. These overpayments can be claimed back from you. But if the overpayment is due to an 'official error' then it should not be recovered unless you could 'reasonably have been expected to realise that it was an overpayment'.

An overpayment can only be recovered from the person who caused the overpayment. It used to be that overpayments would be recovered from landlords receiving HB and this had the effect of causing rent arrears. Now, they can only be recovered when the landlord knew about your circumstances and did not tell the council.[53]

Discretionary housing payments[54]

Your local council can award Discretionary Housing Payments (DHP) if they think that you need extra financial assistance to meet your housing costs. DHPs are discretionary so you cannot insist on one. The amount of DHP and the period it is granted for are also discretionary. There are limits to the amount that can be paid to you by the council and they are not a long-term solution. You cannot appeal to an independent tribunal about a discretionary decision but you can ask the council to look at their decision again if you do not agree with it.

DHPs can be particularly useful if you don't qualify for maximum HB, if you have non-dependant deductions or you are a private tenant and your rent has been restricted.

Extended payments of Housing Benefit

If you have received Income Support, income-based Jobseeker's Allowance or Incapacity Benefit for at least 26 weeks and your entitlement stops because you have started work or increased your hours of work to 16 or more a week, you can qualify for up to four weeks' payment of maximum Housing Benefit. To receive this, it is very important that you tell either Jobcentre Plus or the Housing Benefit service within four weeks of starting the job or increasing your hours. If you just stop signing on as unemployed, you will not receive this money.

Challenging decisions – appeals and the ombudsman

Your local council must send you a written notice about the decision it makes on your HB claim. If you do not qualify for HB, the notice will say why not. If you want more information about how your HB was worked out, you can write to your local authority asking for a written statement. You have the right to ask your local authority to reconsider their decision on almost all matters relating to your HB.

If you disagree with the council decision write to them, stating that you wish to appeal against their decision and stating the reason why. After you appeal the local council will consider changing their decision in your favour. If they don't then it will be forwarded to an independent tribunal who can submit their own decision. The appeal will be heard by an independent tribunal and they can make a decision on your case. The tribunal is usually just one person and is not a court. You don't have to attend the tribunal, although you stand more chance of winning if you do. You must appeal within one month of the decision being sent out. You can get more information from www.tribunals.gov.uk . If you don't want to appeal just write and ask them to reconsider it.

The Ombudsman

You can complain to the Ombudsman if you feel the council administered your claim unfairly or caused unreasonable delays. This is separate from the appeal system. Get information on complaining from the local library or advice centre or by going to www.lgo.org.uk .

Support for young people who are homeless

What is homelessness?

If you do not have a home, or will lose it within 28 days, then you are homeless. This can mean that you are sleeping on a friend's sofa, living in a squat or sleeping on the street. You can also be considered legally homeless if your accommodation is unsuitable, for example if you are suffering from or at risk of abuse, if your accommodation poses a risk to your health or if you simply can't afford to pay for the accommodation without sacrificing essentials such as heating and food.

Young people, housing assistance and the law

If you are homeless you are entitled to housing assistance from your local authority housing department. You can do this by making a homeless application, as is your right under the Housing Act 1996.[55] You are specifically entitled to housing assistance, under the Homelessness Act 2002, which deems 16-17 year olds to have priority need and therefore be entitled to immediate accommodation.[56]

You are almost certainly considered to be eligible for housing assistance if you are a UK citizen and have not recently spent time living abroad,[57] and the law states that there is a clear obligation for your local authority to provide you with accommodation whilst they investigate your situation[58] as well as after your application has been approved. Ideally you should apply to the local authority where you have been living the most in the last five years. If you are fleeing harassment or violence this may not be possible, and it is illegal for another local authority, to which you do not have a local connection, to refuse you assistance. However if you do go to another local authority, they may transfer you back to the authority that you came from later on in the application process.

However, assistance can later be denied if the council feels that you are not homeless, not eligible or intentionally homeless. If the local authority finds you intentionally homeless or not eligible or not homeless then they can relinquish responsibility for housing you. However as with a decision of eligibility and homelessness you can request a review of the local authority's decision within 28 days of notification.[59] The local authority has a duty to place you in accommodation such as a hostel or Bed and Breakfast whilst its investigation is taking place.

Making a homeless application can often be frustrating, time-consuming and confusing and does not always lead to accommodation being immediately obtained, despite the legislation. You should always approach a housing advice organisation such as Shelter or your local Citizens Advice Bureau to advise and support you in making a housing application, particularly if you do not gain accommodation quickly or a negative decision is given.

Social Services Assistance with homelessness

There is a second route for 16-17 year olds to gain accommodation from their local authority – through social services. The Children Act 1989 lays down the duties placed upon local authorities and also gives them powers to help 'children in need'. Your local social services department has a duty to find you accommodation provided you can prove that your wellbeing is threatened by your present homelessness.[60] If you feel that you are in this situation you can phone your local social services department and request an interview to discuss your needs.[61] Taking this route means that often attempts are made to mediate with your family, but your opinions should always be considered in this process.

Social services do have limited access to accommodation and may well approach the housing department anyway. However, if you have been unable to gain accommodation through a homeless application under the Homelessness Act 2002 you may want to ask your local social services department as well as a local support agency for help.

Young people with involvement in the care system

If you have spent more than 13 weeks since the age of 14 in care (meaning you have been placed by social services into the care of foster parents, a children's home, charity or local authority) then you are entitled, under The Children Leaving Care Act 2000, to receive ongoing support from social services, including help in gaining accommodation.[62]

While you still may have to make a homeless application under the Homelessness Act 2002 your leaving care package will allocate you a personal adviser to support you with this.[63] The social services appointed personal adviser will also support you with living independently, filling in forms and setting up a package involving other agencies to help you to reach your goals.[64] As a care leaver you are legally entitled to this support, which is specifically designed for you. As soon as you become, or feel you are at risk of becoming homeless you should contact social services, ideally the department that looked after you originally, informing them of your situation. If you are unhappy with the service you have received, for example if you remain homeless, then you have the right to request a review.

Rough sleeping

As a 16-17 year old the legislation mentioned so far is designed to prevent the circumstances arising that would lead to your having to sleep rough. However, if you do find yourself in this situation, at whatever time of day or night, your local housing and social services departments have emergency out-of-hours phone access. If you can't find these numbers in the phone book then you can phone the homeless charity Shelter on their specialist freephone shelter line (0808 800 4444). You can also access support during office hours from your local Connexions branch, homeless day centre, and Citizens Advice Bureau and/or social services department. Finding accommodation should become your priority if you are homeless, and explaining your circumstances to your school, college, benefits office or employer may help you to prioritise.

Endnotes

1   Reg 33 Social Security (Claims and Payments) Regulations 1987

2   S 72 (1) (a) Social Security Contributions and Benefits Act 1992

3   S 72 (1) (b) Social Security Contributions and Benefits Act 1992

4   S 72 (4) (a) Social Security Contributions and Benefits Act 1992

5   S 73 (1) (d) Social Security Contributions and Benefits Act 1992

6   S 73 (1) (a) & (2) &(3) Social Security Contributions and Benefits Act 1992

7   S 72 (2) & S 73 (9) Social Security Contributions and Benefits Act 1992

8   S 72(8). Social Security Contributions and Benefits Act 1992 & Regs 9, 10 & 12A Social Security (Disability Living Allowance) Regulations 1991

9   S 30A (1) (b) & (2A) Social Security Contributions and Benefits Act 1992

10 Reg 17 Social Security (Incapacity Benefit) Regulations 1994

11 S 171 Contributions and Benefits Act 1992 and Reg 4 Social Security (Incapacity for Work) (General) Regulations 1995

12 Reg 25 Social Security (Incapacity for Work) (General) Regulations 1995

13 Reg 25 & Schedule Social Security (Incapacity for Work) (General) Regulations 1995

14 Regs 10, 13, 14 & 27 Social Security (Incapacity for Work) (General) Regulations 1995

15 Reg 27 Social Security (Incapacity for Work) (General) Regulations 1995 and also see: Howker v Secretary of State for Work and Pensions[2002] EWCA Civ 1623 & CIB/26/2004 & CSIB/33/2004

16 Reg 13A Social Security (Incapacity for Work) (General) Regulations 1995

17 Regs 16 & 17 Social Security (Incapacity for Work) (General) Regulations 1995

18 Reg. 55 Jobseeker's Allowance Regulations 1996

19 Reg. 24 Jobseeker's Allowance Regulations 1996

20 S 29 Children (Scotland) Act 1995

21 Reg 7 Children (Leaving Care Act) 2000 Regulations & Guidance & Reg. 9 (The Support and Assistance of Young people Leaving Care (Scotland) Regulations 2003

22 Para 19B (4) Schedule 2 Children Act 1989 & Reg 8 The Support and Assistance of Young People Leaving Care (Scotland) Regulations 2003

23 Reg. 7 The Children (Leaving Care) (England) Regulations 2001 & Schedule 2 The Support and Assistance of Young People Leaving Care (Scotland) Regulations 2003

[24] S 17 Children Act 1989 & S 22 Children (Scotland) Act 1995

[25] Att Gen ex rel Tilley v London Borough of Wandsworth [1981] 1AER 1162

[26] A v London Borough of Lambeth. [2001] EWCA 1624

[27] For example, see R v London Borough of Hillingdon ex p Berhe and others. (2003 EWHC 2075).

[28] DMG JSA/IS 54

[29] S 6 (1) Children Leaving Care Act 2000

[30] For all IS & JSA exceptions see Reg 2 The Children (Leaving Care) Social Security Benefits Regulations 2001 and Reg 2(3) The Children (Leaving Care) Social Security Benefits (Scotland) Regulations 2004

[31] Dept of Health Guidance on Schedule 8 The Children (Leaving Care) Social Security Benefits Regulations 2001

[32] Chapter 9 paras 5 - 6 Dept of Health Guidance on The Children (Leaving Care) Social Security Benefits Regulations 2001

[33] Chapter 9. DoH Guidance ibid & Reg.13 (3) The Support and Assistance of Young People Leaving Care (Scotland) Regulations 2003

[34] Regs 16 – 19 The Support and Assistance of Young People Leaving Care (Scotland) Regulations 2003 and S 5B Social Work Scotland Act 1968

[35] S 23C. Children Act 1989 Ss. 29 & 30 Children (Scotland) Act 1995

[36] S 24 Children Act 1989

[37] Sch 9 para 28, Income Support (General) Regulations 1987, Sch 7 para 29 Jobseeker's Allowance Regulations, Sch 5 para 28 Housing Benefit (General) Regulations 2006

[38] Reg 2(1) Housing Benefit (General) Regulations 2006 – see definition of 'young individual'

[39] See DWP Housing Benefit Circular to local authorities, No A30/95 para 17 iv

[40] Reg 56 Housing Benefit (General) Regulations 2006

[41] Reg 9 Housing Benefit (General) Regulations 2006

[42] Reg 12 Housing Benefit (General) Regulations 2006

[43] The Rent Officers (Housing Benefit Functions Order) 1997/1984 & reg 13 Housing Benefit (General) Regulations 2006

[44] Reg 3 Housing Benefit (General) Regulations 2006

[45] Reg 74 Housing Benefit (General) Regulations 2006

[46] Reg 7 Housing Benefit (General) Regulations 2006

[47] Reg 7 Housing Benefit (General) Regulations 2006

[48] Reg 83(12) Housing Benefit (General) Regulations 2006

[49] Reg 86 Housing Benefit (General) Regulations 2006

[50] Regs 89(2), 90(1) & 91(3) Housing Benefit (General) Regulations 2006

[51] Reg 93 Housing Benefit (General) Regulations 2006

[52] Reg 99 Housing Benefit (General) Regulations 2006

[53] Reg 101(2) Housing Benefit (General) Regulations 2006

[54] The Discretionary Financial Assistance Regulations 2001

[55] S 182 Housing Act 1996

[56] The Homelessness (Priority Need for Accommodation) (England) Order 2002; SI 2002 No.2051

[57] Allocation of Housing and Homelessness (Eligibility) (England) Regulations 2006, SI no. 1294

[58] S 188 Housing Act 1996

[59] S 202 of the Housing Act 1996

[60] SS 17 and 20 of the Children Act 1989

[61] R v Barnet LBC ex parte G: R v Lambeth LBC ex parte W: R v Lambeth ex parte A [2003] UKHL 57

[62] S 23B(8) Children Act 1989 as amended by s.2 Children (Leaving Care) Act 2000

[63] LA has a legal duty to assess relevant child's needs - Part 2 para 19B(4), Sch.2 and S 23B(3) Children Act 1989, as amended by SS 1 and 2 Children (Leaving Care) Act 2000.

[64] SS 23B(3) and 23E Children Act 1989, as amended by SS 2 and 3 Children (Leaving Care) Act 2000 and S 23B(2) AND 23D Children Act 1989, as amended by SS 2 and 3 Children (Leaving Care) Act 2000

Financial support for young people in particular circumstances

6 Moving into work

Equalities legislation

UK employment law gives all employees protection against discrimination in the workplace on the grounds of sex, pregnancy, race, age, disability, sexual orientation, religion or belief.

The following section provides you with some more detailed information about age discrimination, the rights that you have under UK law, what to do if you feel you have been the victim of discrimination and details of where you can access further information and support. For more information about equalities legislation generally, see *Inclusion*'s "Working in the UK: Newcomer's Handbook".

Age discrimination

Although age discrimination is something usually associated with older people, it can take place against young people too.

What is the law?

The Employment Equality (Age) Regulations 2006

This new legislation is there to protect everyone, young and old, from discrimination in the workplace on the grounds of age.

The legislation bans employers from discriminating on the grounds of age when:

- deciding whom to employ;
- offering the terms of employment;

- providing opportunities for promotion, training, transfer or any other benefit.[1]

The new rights and responsibilities associated with these regulations apply to all employers.

For young people this is important because it means that employers cannot legally impose a lower age limit when recruiting unless this age limit can be objectively justified or imposed by law.

Exceptions to the law

There are some important exceptions in this legislation. These are the ones that might be most relevant to you.

National Minimum Wage

It is not unlawful for employees to receive different levels of pay based on their age if these differences are in line with the National Minimum Wage rates for young workers.[2] This means, for example, that those aged 22 or over are legally entitled to earn more than those aged 21 or under.

Positive action

It is legal for employers to offer training, facilities or generally encourage people from a particular age group if doing so is intended to compensate for employment-based disadvantages associated with people of that particular age group.[3]

Exception for provision of certain benefits based on length of service

Employers are allowed to provide employees with benefits linked to their length of service.[4] This could mean that someone who has been working for your employer longer than you might be entitled to receive extra benefits, like higher pension contributions.

Employment rights

Employment contract

You are legally entitled to be provided with a contract from your employer within two months of the start of a new job. This contract sets out the nature of your job and any terms and conditions associated with it. Your contract should include the following information:

- your name and that of your employer;
- the date employment started;
- your rate of pay;
- your hours of work and holiday entitlement;
- the title and description of your job and your place of work;
- your notice period;
- details of an employer's grievance and disciplinary procedure;
- if the employment is not permanent, the period for which it is expected to continue, or if it is fixed term, the date on which it is to end.[5]

Pay

Under the National Minimum Wage regulations, all workers are entitled to be paid at least the National Minimum Wage rate for each hour that they work.[6]

The rates from 1st October 2006 are:

Population	Rate per hour
Workers over the age of 22	£5.35
Workers aged 18-21	£4.45
Workers aged 16-17	£3.30

From October 2007 these rates will rise to: £3.40 for workers aged 16-17, £4.60 for workers aged 18-21 and £5.52 for workers over the age of 22.

These rates are usually updated in October of each year. You can find out what the current National Minimum Wage is by visiting: http://www.hmrc.gov.uk/nmw.

These regulations are enforced by HM Revenue & Customs. If you would like more information or advice or would like to make a complaint you can call the National Minimum Wage helpline: 0845 6000 678.

Working time regulations

Any employee aged 16-18 cannot usually be made to work more than eight hours a day or 40 hours a week. These hours can't be averaged over a longer period. There are some exceptions to this legislation including if you work for one of a few excluded sectors or if you are offered compensatory rest.[7]

Your employer may ask you to opt out of these working time regulations. This means signing a form which says you are happy to work longer hours. However, an employer cannot legally force you to opt out: it should be your free choice. If you do opt out, you can also change your mind at any time and request to be covered by working time regulations again.

Your employer is breaking the law if they treat you unfairly or sack you because you refuse to opt out. If you think your employer has treated you unfairly you might be able to take them to an employment tribunal. You can find out more about your rights and the steps you can take if you have been unfairly treated by visiting the TUC webite: http://www.tuc.org.uk/tuc/rights_main.cfm

Statutory Sick Pay

If you have to take more than four days off work because of illness, you may be entitled to sick pay. The government sets a minimum amount of sick pay you should receive. This is called Statutory Sick Pay (SSP).

You are entitled to be paid SSP for up to a maximum of 28 weeks.

In order to qualify to receive Statutory Sick Pay, you must be aged above 16 and be earning enough to pay National Insurance contributions (before tax and National Insurance an average of £87.00 a week).

If you meet these criteria, then you are entitled to receive the standard rate of £70.05 a week for the period for which you are absent from work because of sickness.[8]

You should be aware that some companies are more generous and pay more than this minimum amount. You should check your contractual information to see if this is the case.

Holiday entitlement

Currently, under the Working Time Regulations, everyone is legally entitled to a minimum of four weeks' (20 days') paid holiday a year.[9] However, from October 2007 this will rise to 24 days and will rise again in 2008 to 28 days.

However, a week's holiday means you get as many days off as you work in a normal working week.

This means that the actual amount of paid holiday entitlement you receive depends on how many days you work.

For example, if you work five days a week, you work twenty days in four weeks, so you currently get twenty days' paid holiday each leave year. If you work three days a week, you work 12 days in four weeks so you get 12 days' paid holiday each leave year.

You should always check your contract or employment handbook to see if your employer offers more generous holiday entitlements.

The Citizens Advice Bureau website – Advice Guide, has lots of useful information on your employment rights. You can find a more detailed explanation of holiday pay entitlements at:

http://www.adviceguide.org.uk/index/life/employment/holidays_and_holiday_pay.htm

Maternity leave

All female employees have the right to 26 weeks of 'ordinary maternity leave' and 26 weeks of 'additional maternity leave' – making a year in total.

This right belongs to all pregnant women, providing they meet the 15 week notification requirement outlined below. It does not matter how long you have been with your employer, how many hours you work or how much you are paid.

You should tell your employer that you are pregnant and intend to take maternity leave at least 15 weeks before the beginning of the week your baby is due.

You will need to tell your employer that you are pregnant, when the baby is due and when you want to start your maternity leave.

You can start maternity leave any time from 11 weeks before the beginning of the week when your baby is due.[10]

http://www.direct.gov.uk/en/Parents/Workingparents/DG_10039631

Statutory Maternity Pay (SMP)

From 1 April 2007, providing you have been employed by the same employer without a break for at least 26 weeks into the 15th week before the week your baby is due and earning more than £87 a week, you are entitled to receive SMP.

SMP is 90 per cent of your average weekly earnings for the first six weeks of your maternity leave. For the following 33 weeks, you are entitled to receive either £112.75 or 90 per cent of your average earnings, whichever is less.

This is usually paid to you by your employer in the same way as your normal wages.[11]

Some employers have their own maternity leave arrangements which may be more generous. You can find out if this is the case by looking at your employment contract.

Other benefits

If you do not qualify to receive SMP you may be able to claim Maternity Allowance through Jobcentre Plus. Maternity Allowance is paid at the same rate as SMP.

There are a number of other benefits which expectant and new mothers may be entitled to receive. These include Child Trust Funds, Sure Start Maternity grants, Child Benefit, free prescriptions and dental treatment and Tax Credits.

You can find out more about Maternity Allowances and other benefits by visiting: http://www.direct.gov.uk/en/Parents/Workingparents/ DG_10029290

Paternity leave

You are entitled to paid paternity leave if you meet the following criteria:

- You are the biological father of the baby and/or the mother's husband, civil partner or partner.
- You have worked continuously for the same employer for 26 weeks by the 25th week of pregnancy and will continue to do so up to the birth of the child.

If you meet these two criteria, you are entitled to up to two weeks paternity leave. This time off must be taken in one go. It cannot be taken as odd days or as two separate weeks.

If you would like to take paternity leave, you will need to tell your employer before the end of the 25th week of pregnancy.

Statutory Paternity Pay (SPP)

While you are on paternity leave you may be entitled to SPP of £112.75 a week, or 90% of your average weekly earnings if this is below £112.75.

To claim SPP you must be earning over £87 a week. You must also notify your employer that you would like to be paid SPP at least 28 days before you begin paternity leave.

Other benefits

If you do not qualify for SPP because you are not earning more than £87 a week you may be entitled to receive other benefits. These include: Income Support, Housing Benefit, Council Tax Benefit and Tax Credits.

You can find out more about your rights in relation to paternity leave and pay by visiting: http://www.direct.gov.uk/en/Parents/Workingparents/DG_10029398

Accidents or diseases which are related to work or training

If you have an accident, or contract a 'prescribed disease' (PD), in the course of your work or work-based learning and as a result you are still suffering some disability 15 weeks later, you may qualify for Industrial Injuries Disablement Benefit (IIDB).

(The full list of prescribed diseases is available in the CPAG Welfare Benefits and Tax Credits Handbook, the Disability Rights Handbook and there is some information in DWP leaflet No SD 6 – "Ill or Disabled because of a disease or deafness caused by work?")

Employed status learners can make a claim to IIDB through Jobcentre Plus.

Non-employed status learners can make a claim to IIDB through the Analogous Industrial Injuries Scheme at the Department for Work and Pensions – call 01977 464094.

The Analogous Industrial Injuries Scheme (AIIS) is a discretionary scheme, which uses the same guidance and the same doctors and pays benefits at the same rates as Jobcentre Plus. It covers non-employed learners on work-based learning that is funded by the LSC or by the Department for Work and Pensions (DWP). It does not cover work experience placements, or any non-employed status learning that might be arranged privately, through schools, or through Further Education Colleges.

How to claim

If you have an accident or contract a prescribed disease as a result of your work you should inform your employer and learning provider as soon as possible. Your learning provider must then send a report to the Learning and Skills Council (LSC).

If you do not have employed status, the LSC will send this report to the AIIS team, which will write to you with information about the scheme and invite you to start the claims process.

If you have employed status, it is up to you to start the claims process by contacting your local Jobcentre Plus office, or you can download a form from the Jobcentre Plus website.

It is important to follow the instructions that come with the forms as delay in making a claim may result in the loss of some benefit.

Making a claim for Disablement Benefit does not stop you from taking legal action against your employer or training provider. However, compensation awarded by the court may be reduced by the amount of benefits you receive. DWP booklet GL27, Compensation and social security benefits, gives more detail.

What happens next

A Decision Maker (DM) from within Jobcentre Plus or from the AIIS team, depending on your status, will decide if your accident counts as an industrial accident, and you will be sent a copy of the decision. If your accident is accepted you can make a claim for benefit. Before a decision is made on your entitlement to benefit you will be asked to attend a medical examination that will be carried out by one or two independent doctors near to where you live.

If you have contracted a 'prescribed disease' a decision will not normally be given until you have attended a medical examination.

If the doctor's assessment of your disability is at least 14% IIDB is paid at a rate determined by the extent of your disability. You don't need to show that you are permanently disabled as awards can range from a few months to a lifetime. IIDB can be paid 15 weeks after the date of an accident, or the date a PD was contracted (Even if you have continued with your training during this time, you can still apply for IIDB.) IIDB does not depend on National Insurance contributions.

If you are awarded IIDB at 100% and need daily care and attention, you may be entitled to payment of Constant Attendance Allowance.

If you have received a means-tested benefit e.g. Income Support (IS) or income-based Job Seekers Allowance (JSA) since your accident , you may not be entitled to receive some or any arrears of disablement benefits. IIDB counts as income for income-based benefits. Therefore if you are getting a means-tested benefit now, this may be reduced by the amount of IIDB payable. Payment of IIDB is not affected by Incapacity Benefit, Statutory Sick Pay, Training Allowance or earnings.

IIDB Benefit Rates

Assessed % Disablement	Weekly rate of benefit if aged under 18 with no dependants
100%	£80.70
90%	£72.63
80%	£64.56
70%	£56.49
60%	£48.42
50%	£40.35
40%	£32.28
30%	£24.21
20%	£16.14

Appeals

To appeal against a DM s decision you should follow the advice on the decision letter. Take note of any time limits for making an appeal. You may be asked to attend a further medical examination to enable a fair decision to be made on your claim.

You can find out more about AIIS by visiting: http://www.jobcentreplus.gov.uk/jcp/Partners/Allowancesandbenefits/Dev_009942.xml.html

Tax Credits and young people

You may be entitled to claim Tax Credits. There are two types of Tax Credit: Child Tax Credit (CTC) and Working Tax Credit (WTC) and the main features are:

- You must be at least 16;
- The Tax Credits are administered by Her Majesty's Revenue and Customs (HMRC) rather than the Department for Work and Pensions;
- Entitlement is based on your gross annual income rather than net weekly income;
- There is no capital limit but any income above £300 a year from taxable savings is counted as income;
- If you have children and you make a new claim for Income Support (IS) or income-based Jobseeker's Allowance (ibJSA) you will not have personal allowances and premiums for children included when calculating these benefits. You will receive CTC instead. Any elements for adults and housing costs (such as mortgages) will still be met by IS/ibJSA. Existing IS/ibJSA claimants with children will have been transferred onto CTC by the end of 2007;
- Tax Credits are paid on top of other benefits, but they count as income for means-tested benefits (but if you are receiving Tax Credits instead of the child elements of IS/ibJSA, they are ignored as income). IS and ibJSA are calculated on the basis of how much tax credit you are entitled to. Housing Benefit is based on the amount of tax credit actually being paid;
- If you get tax credits, you might get passported benefits such as free school meals, prescriptions and dental care;
- If you receive WTC, you may get help with up to 80% of your childcare costs;
- A claim for Tax Credits by a lone parent will not trigger Child Support Agency involvement;
- Any maintenance which is received is completely ignored as income;
- Couples must make a joint claim;
- Certain other types of income are ignored – for example, maintenance, training allowances, Disability Living Allowance, Housing Benefit, Child Benefit, Guardian's Allowance, IS & ibJSA, reimbursement of expenses 'wholly exclusively and necessarily' involved in your employment, the first £100 of Statutory Maternity

Pay, Maternity Allowance, Statutory Sick Pay;

Child Tax Credit

Child Tax Credit is designed to provide additional support for families with children. Depending on individual circumstances it is payable for children and for 16, 17, 18 and 19 year olds still living with their families, provided they are in full-time non-advanced education. It is based on the family income.

If you are 16 or 17, you can receive CTC in your own right if:

- You have main responsibility for a child under 16 or one under 20 who is in full-time non-advanced education if they normally live with you;
- You are present and ordinarily resident in Great Britain;
- You are not a 'person subject to immigration control';

Child Tax Credit is payable to the person who has main caring responsibility for at least one child or qualifying young person. You do not need to be the parent of the child you are responsible for. It is awarded until the end of the tax year unless there are significant changes in circumstances.

Tax Credits your parents claim for you

See pages 24-30

Working Tax Credit

Working tax credit is paid by HMRC to people with or without families who are on a low income.

If you are 16 or 17, you can receive WTC if:

- you (or your partner if you have one) are responsible for a child and one of you is employed for at least 16 hours a week, or
- you have a physical or mental disability which means that you are at

a disadvantage in finding or keeping work and you either receive or have recently received certain disability-related benefits, and you are employed for at least 16 hours a week;

- your partner is aged at least 25 and they are employed for at least 30 hours a week;
- you are present and ordinarily resident in Great Britain;
- you are not a 'person subject to immigration control'.

Childcare costs

It is possible for HMRC to include 80% of your childcare costs in your WTC calculation. However, you can't receive more than £175 a week for one child and £300 a week for two or more children. You must also meet some other conditions:

- The childcare must be 'relevant childcare' – in other words, a childminder, nursery, after-school club, breakfast club, childcare provided in your own home by an approved childminder (but not if they are a close relative).
- If you are single, you must work for at least 16 hours a week. If you have a partner, both of you must work for least 16 hours a week.
- If you a have a partner and only one of you works for at least 16 hours a week, you can still get help with childcare costs if the other person is:
    - in hospital or prison, or
    - 'incapacitated' and receiving a benefit because of this.

You must tell HMRC if your childcare costs go up or down by £10 a week or more for four or more weeks. If you don't, they may make you pay a £300 penalty.

How much Tax Credit?

You receive various elements in your Tax Credit calculation depending on your circumstances. If you have a child with a disability or you receive a benefit for disability or long-term sickness, you may qualify for higher amounts.

If your income is less than £5,220 and you qualify for WTC, you will receive maximum tax credits.

If your income is more than this threshold, your maximum Tax Credit gradually reduces by 37p for each pound that your income is above the threshold. If you only qualify for CTC, you receive the maximum if your income is less than £14,495 (or if you receive IS/ibJSA) and then it reduces by 37p for each pound that your income is above that level until you are left with the family element of CTC of £545 a year.

You then keep this until your income reaches £50,000 when it then reduces by 6.67p for each pound that your income is above that level.

The calculation is also done by working out your 'relevant period'. Normally this will be a full year, but if you go onto tax credits later in the year, your relevant period will be reduced to take account of this. Also, if your childcare costs or your household composition changes, HMRC works out a new relevant period to adjust your Tax Credit entitlement.

The Tax Credit Ready Reckoner

There is a simple guide to working out your tax credit entitlement available on the HMRC website: http://www.hmrc.gov.uk/taxcredits/reckoner.pdf .

Overpayments

Because they are based on annual income, some people may find that they are paid too much tax credit if their income rises or their entitlement reduces (for example, childcare costs decreasing by more than £10 a week for more than 4 weeks).

If your income increases by up to £25,000 a year, HMRC will ignore this and only count any increase above £25,000 a year.

If you do find that you have been overpaid, the law gives HMRC a general discretion to waive recovery of an overpayment.[12] They will also not recover the overpayment if it was their fault and you couldn't be reasonably expected to realise this or if repaying any overpayment would cause you hardship.[13] HMRC will not consider waiving recovery unless you ask them to. If they refuse to waive recovery, you can complain to the HMRC adjudicator (www.adjudicatorsoffice.gov.uk) and you can ask your MP to complain to the Parliamentary Ombudsman. Sometimes it may be possible to take a form of legal action known as judicial review.

How to claim

You can get a tax credit claim form (TC600) at any Jobcentre if you are entering work after being out of work (and they should help you to complete it if you ask), or by phoning HMRC on 0845 300 3900.

Your claim can be backdated for up to three months before you claimed. If you were entitled, you do not need to show any special reasons and you should also apply for backdating if you think you missed out.

Healthy Start scheme

This was introduced in November 2006 to replace the scheme of free milk for people on very low incomes. It provides vouchers worth £2.80 towards a range of healthier foods including fresh milk, infant formula milk and fresh fruit and vegetables. The vouchers may be used in a wide range of shops, including supermarkets, chemists and markets.

You are eligible for Healthy Start vouchers if you are pregnant or have a child under the age of four and if you also:

- are pregnant and aged under 18 years of age (in this case, you do not have to be receiving any benefit to qualify) or
- receive Income Support, or income-based Jobseeker's Allowance, or
- receive Child Tax Credit (but not Working Tax Credit) and have an annual family income of below £14,495.

How many vouchers are paid?

One voucher a week is paid if you're pregnant plus two vouchers for each baby aged under one and one voucher for each child aged over one and under four. For more details see www.healthystart.nhs.uk.

Endnotes

[1] Employment Equality (Age) Regulations 2006 (7.1&7.2)

[2] Employment Equality (Age) Regulations 2006 (31)

[3] Employment Equality (Age) Regulations 2006 (29)

[4] Employment Equality (Age) Regulations 2006 (32)

[5] Employment Rights Act 1996 (s 1). Available online, http://www.opsi.gov.uk/acts/acts1996/1996018.htm (retrieved 14.03.07)

[6] The National Minimum Wage Regulations 1999. Available online, http://www.opsi.gov.uk/acts/acts1996/1996018.htm (retrieved 14.03.07)

[7] The Working Time (Amendment) Regulations 2002. Available online, http://www.opsi.gov.uk/si/si2002/20023128.htm (retrieved 14.03.07)

[8] http://www.dwp.gov.uk/lifeevent/benefits/statutory_sick_pay.asp (retrieved 14.03.07)

[9] Working Time Regulations 1998 (s 13). Available online, http://www.opsi.gov.uk/si/si1998/19981833.htm (retrieved 14.03.07)

[10] http://www.direct.gov.uk/en/Parents/Workingparents/DG_10039631 (retrieved 14.03.07)

[11] http://www.direct.gov.uk/en/Bfsl1/BenefitsAndFinancialSupport/DG_10018741 (retrieved 14.03.07)

[12] Sections 28 & 29 Tax Credits Act 2002.

[13] HMRC leaflet COP 26: What happens if we have paid you too much tax credit

7 Appendix 1

Standard letter to support Income Support estrangement and
Jobseeker's Allowance severe hardship claims. Reproduced from
www.neilbateman.co.uk with permission

[TO BE USED ON HEADED PAPER]

To Jobcentre Plus	
Address	
Postcode	

Dear Sir or Madam

Re: [Full name]

[Address]

[NINo]

[DOB]

The above named young person has made a claim for a) Jobseeker's
Allowance because of severe hardship b) Income Support while in
full-time education because, of necessity, they live away from and are
estranged from their parents/carers and no one is acting in their place
c) Jobseeker's Allowance during the Child Benefit Extension Period
because, of necessity, they are living away from their parents or anyone

acting in their place and they are estranged from their parents/carers [Delete which sentences do not apply]. I enclose a copy of their consent for us to act for them.

[To be used for estrangement cases only] Estrangement implies emotional disharmony, where there is no desire to have any prolonged contact with the parents or the parents feel similarly towards the young person. It is possible to be estranged even though parents are providing some financial support or the young person still has some contact with them (based on Commissioner's decision R(SB) 2/87). As can be seen from this binding Commissioner's decision, it is sufficient only that one party feels estranged. There is no legal requirement therefore for the parents to be contacted to confirm that they also feel estranged.

The following is confirmation of the young person's estrangement/ emotional disharmony/being alienated in affection with parents/carers: [Give examples/evidence]

Parents/carers should not be contacted by DWP staff for verification, because claimants' statements do not require corroboration unless their evidence is inherently improbably or self-contradictory (please refer to R(SB) 33/85 and R(I) 2/51). This is set out in internal DWP Guidance in IS Bulletin 04-07 "Estranged Young People aged 16-19 claiming Income Support" and also in DWP Guidance "Making a Severe Hardship Decision" (available on the Jobcentre Plus Intranet). These two guidance documents state that: "The Young Person should be believed unless their statement is self-contradictory or inherently improbable... There is no rule in law that corroboration of the customer's own evidence is necessary and it is seldom safe to reject evidence solely because the customer's demeanour does not inspire confidence in their truthfulness."

In addition, I wish to inform you of the following risks associated with contacting parents: [Give reasons why contact is inappropriate or delete if this is not relevant]

[Use only for JSA SHP claims]. This person will experience severe hardship for the following reasons: [Give details and delete those which are not relevant]

Lack of financial resources:

Risk to health:

Has insecure accommodation:

Possible loss of accommodation:

Has debts:

Carer/parent has financial pressures:

Carer/parent unable/unwilling to adequately support financially:

The young person or a member of their family would be vulnerable without payment:

The young person is pregnant:

Others:

Please send me a copy of your decision and please also direct any further enquires via me.

Yours faithfully

[Name and job title]

7

Appendix 2

Social security and tax credit rates for young people 2007-08

MEANS-TESTED BENEFITS

Income Support & income-based Jobseeker's Allowance

Personal Allowances

Single person, under 18	lower rate	35.65
	higher rate	46.85
Single person, aged 18 – 24		46.85
Single person, aged 25 +		59.15
Lone parent, under 18	lower rate	35.65
	higher rate	46.85
Lone parent, aged 18 +		59.15
Couple, both under 18		35.65 / 46.65 / 70.70
Couple, one under 18		46.65 / 59.15 / 92.80
Couple both 18+		92.80

Premiums

Carer	27.15
Disability, single	25.25
Disability, couple	36.00
Enhanced disability, single person / lone parent	12.30
Enhanced Disability, couple	17.75
Severe Disability, per qualifying person	48.45

Housing Benefit & Council Tax Benefit

As for Income Support / income-based JSA or Pension Credit, except for:

Personal Allowances

Single person, under 18 (n/a for Council Tax Benefit)	46.85
Lone parent, under 18 (n/a for CTB)	46.85
Couple, both under 18 (n/a for CTB)	70.70
Child	47.45

Premiums

Family	16.43
Family, baby rate	10.50

Working Tax Credit (annual rates)

Basic element	1,730
Couple / lone parent	1,700
30 hours element	705
Disability element	2,310
Severe disability element	980
Childcare costs, one child (up to 80%)	max 175(pw)
Childcare costs, two children (up to 80%)	max 300 (pw)

Child Tax Credit (annual rates)

Family element	545
Baby addition	545
Child element	1,845
Disabled child	2,440
Severely disabled child	980

NON MEANS-TESTED BENEFITS

Carer's Allowance

Carer's Allowance	48.65
Adult dependant	29.05

Child Benefit

Only / eldest child	18.10
Per other child	12.10

Disability Living Allowance

Care component	Lowest rate	17.10
	Middle rate	43.15
	Highest rate	64.50
Mobility Component	Lower rate	17.10
	Higher rate	45.00

Incapacity Benefit

Short term	Lower rate	61.35
	Higher rate	72.55
	Long term	83.35
Long term, age addition	Lower rate (35 – 44)	8.55
	Higher rate (under 35)	17.10
Short term, adult dependant		46.90
Long term, adult dependant		48.65

Industrial Injuries Disablement Benefit and Analogous Industrial Injuries Scheme

(Variable depending on % disablement)

Under 18	16.14 – 80.70
Under 18 with dependants	26.34 – 131.70
Aged 18 +	26.34 – 131.70

Jobseeker's Allowance (contribution based)

Under 18	35.65
Aged 18 – 24	46.85
Aged 25 +	59.15

Maternity Allowance

Standard rate	112.75
Adult Dependant	37.90
Statutory Maternity, Paternity & Adoption Pay (standard rate)	112.75
Statutory Sick Pay	72.55

NATIONAL MINIMUM WAGE (per hour)

	Current Rates: Oct '06	Coming rates: Oct '07
Aged 22+	£5.35	£5.52
Aged 18 – 21 or in approved training	£4.45	£4.60
Aged 16 –17	£3.30	£3.40

Useful contacts

Useful books about benefit rights

Welfare Benefits & Tax Credits Handbook 2007/08
(Child Poverty Action Group)

Child Support Handbook 2007/2008 (CPAG)

Lone Parent Handbook 2006/07 (One Parent Families)

Disability Rights Handbook 2007-2008 (Disability Alliance)

Benefits

Department for Work and Pensions
The Department for Work and Pensions can be contacted at
www.dwp.gov.uk.

Jobs

Department for Work and Pensions

The Department for Work and Pensions can be contacted at
www.dwp.gov.uk

Directgov: Employment

This website offers help and advice for anyone who is in work or looking
for work and training.

www.direct.gov.uk/en/Employment

Jobcentre Plus

The Jobcentre Plus website is www.jobcentreplus.gov.uk. Details of all local Jobcentre Plus offices can be found here. The website also lists whom you need to contact if you have a complaint, query or suggestion.

If you are a jobseeker, you can call Jobseeker Direct: 0845 6060 234

Under-Eighteens Support Team (Severe hardship JSA claims) can be reached on tel. 01253 848000.

need2know

This government website for 13-19 year olds provides information on for young people on work, learning, housing, health and money. http://www.need2know.co.uk/

Children and Young People

Careers Scotland

This service aims to equip people living in Scotland with the skills to make well-informed career decisions – use the website or call: 0845 8 502 502.
www.careers-scotland.org.uk/

Careers Wales/Gyrfa Cymru

This website has targeted advice for different age groups, including specific careers information and advice for 16 – 19 year olds. http://www.careerswales.com/

Child Poverty Action Group (CPAG)

CPAG promotes action for the relief, directly or indirectly, of poverty among children and families with children. It works to ensure that those on low incomes get their full entitlement to welfare benefits. It published several books detailing the current information on welfare rights and social policy issues. Contact details:

94 White Lion Street, London N1 9PF
Tel: 020 7837 7979   Fax: 020 7837 6414
Email: staff@cpag.org.uk
Website: http://www.cpag.org.uk/

Child Support Agency

The Child Support Agency exists to ensure that, where an application for child maintenance has been made, parents who live apart contribute financially to the upkeep of their children. You can find out more by visiting their website: www.csa.gov.uk/. You can also contact their national helpline: 08457 133 133

Connexions

The Connexions Service was set up to give all 13-19 year olds in England a better start in life, providing integrated information, advice and guidance. Visit the Connexions website: www.connexions-direct.com/. Alternatively, you can contact an adviser by calling: 080 800 13 2 19.

CPAG in Scotland

Unit 09 Ladywell
94 Duke Street
Glasgow G4 0UW
General queries: 0141 5552 3303

Advice line

(Advice agencies in Scotland only, Tuesday and Wednesday 10am-12 noon)

Tel: 0141 552 0552   Fax: 0141 552 4404
Email: staff@cpagscotland.org.uk
Website: www.cpag.org.uk/

Directgov: 14 to 19

This part of the Directgov website aims to help you make sense of the choices you need to make between 14 and 19.
http://www.direct.gov.uk/en/EducationAndLearning/14To19

The Prince's Trust

The Prince's Trust offers a range of services to young people (aged 18-30) including educational underachievers, refugees and asylum seekers, unemployed, in/leaving care.

Website: www.princes-trust.org.uk
Email: info@princes-trust.org.uk
Telephone: 0800 842 842

Lone Parents

National Helpline

There is a New Deal for Lone Parents freephone helpline number:
0800 868 868

One Parent Families | Gingerbread

This charity provides help and advice to lone parent families. You can call their advice line: 0800 018 5026, Monday to Friday 9am to 5pm, Wednesdays 9am to 8pm. Or, visit their website for more information:
www.oneparentfamilies.org.uk

Equality

Commission for Equality and Human Rights (CEHR)

CEHR is launching in October 2007.The CEHR will bring together the work of the Commission for Racial Equality (CRE), Disability Rights Commission (DRC) and Equal Opportunities Commission (EOC) . It will enforce equality legislation on age, disability and health, gender, race, religion or belief, sexual orientation or transgender status. The CEHR website is on http://www.cehr.org.uk/

Employment Relations

ACAS

ACAS is the employment relations expert. It can offer free impartial help and information to people experiencing problems with employment issues on its helpline service at 0845 747 747. Visit the ACAS website: www.acas.org.uk/.

ACAS has an office base in seven regions of England. The head office address is:

Brandon House. 180 Borough High Street, London SE1 1LW

Health and Safety Executive (HSE)

The HSE ensures that risks to people's health and safety from work activities are properly controlled. It offers an information line to the public: 0845 345 0055.You can also visit their website for more information: www.hse.gov.uk.

Trades Union Congress

The TUC is the voice of Britain at work. With 71 affiliated unions representing nearly seven million working people from all walks of life, they campaign for a fair deal at work and for social justice at home and abroad.

The TUC is based at:
Congress House, Great Russell Street, London WC1B 3LS
Tel: 020 7636 4030
Website: www.tuc.org.uk

Education and Training

Aimhigher

This website provides information on university applications and finance: http://www.aimhigher.ac.uk/

Apprenticeships

This LSC website is designed to help you decide if a Modern Apprenticeship is for you, and tell you how to apply. http://www.apprenticeships.org.uk/

Department for Children, Schools and Families (DCSF)

is responsible for improving the focus on all aspects of policy affecting children and young people.

Contact the Department by e-mail on info@dcsf.gsi.gov.uk or by telephone on 0870 000 2288.

Directgov: Education

Directgov provides information on GCSEs, NVQs, EMA and higher education. http://www.direct.gov.uk/en/EducationAndLearning/

Learning and Skills Council (LSC)

The LSC is responsible for funding and planning education and training for over-16-year-olds in England.

For general enquiries, contact the LSC helpline on 0870 900 6800 or email info@lsc.gov.uk. If you have a query about provision in your area, there is a comprehensive email list of the 49 local LSCs on the main website at www.lsc.gov.uk.

Educational Grants Advisory Service (EGAS)

EGAS offers guidance and advice on funding for those studying in post-16 education. Call the advice line on 020 7254 6251 or visit the website at http://www.egas-online.org .

Other

Citizens Advice Bureau

The Citizens Advice Bureau (CAB) provide advice on a range of issues. A directory of local telephone numbers is on their website at www.citizensadvice.org.uk.

Refugee Council

If you are a migrant, seek advice from a professional. Initial help for asylum seekers, those with Exceptional Leave to Remain or Humanitarian Protection and refugees can be found at the Refugee Council on 020 7346 6700or online at www.refugeecouncil.org.uk.

Shelter

If you need housing advice, particularly if you are without a home, Shelter offers a freephone number, 0808 800 444, or visit them online at www.shelter.org.uk.

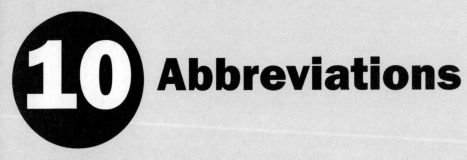

10 Abbreviations

AA	Attendance Allowance
AIIS	Analogous Industrial Injuries Scheme
AMA	Advanced Modern Apprenticeship
CA	Carer's Allowance
CB	Child Benefit
CBEP	Child Benefit Extension Period
CV	Curriculum Vitae
CTB	Council Tax Benefit
CTC	Child Tax Credit
DCSF	Department for Children, Schools and Families
DIUS	Department for Innovation, Universities and Skills
DLA	Disability Living Allowance
DM	Decision Maker
DMG	Decision Maker's Guide
DWP	Department for Work and Pensions
e2e	Entry to Employment
EMA	Education Maintenance Allowance
ETO	Education and Training Opportunities
FE	Further Education
FMA	Foundation Modern Apprenticeship
FTET	Full-time Education and Training
GCE	General Certificate in Education
HB	Housing Benefit

HMRC	Her Majesty's Revenue and Customs
IAP	Intensive Activity Period
IB	Incapacity Benefit
IBJSA	Income-based Jobseeker's Allowance
IIDB	Industrial Injuries Disablement Benefit
IS	Income Support
JSA	Jobseeker's Allowance
LA	Local Authority
LFI	Learning Focused Interview
LSC	Learning and Skills Council
NDLP	New Deal for Lone Parents
NDPA	New Deal personal adviser
NDYP	New Deal for Young People
NI	National Insurance
NVQ	National Vocational Qualification
Ofsted	Office for Standards in Education
PCA	Personal Capability Assessment
SF	Social Fund
SMP	Statutory Maternity Pay
SSP	Statutory Sick Pay
SVQ	Scottish Vocational Qualification
TfW	Training for Work
TIC	Travel to Interview Scheme
UK	United Kingdom
VCE	Vocational Certificates in Education
WBL	Work Based Learning
WBLYP	Work Based Learning for Young People
WFI	Work Focused Interview
WTC	Working Tax Credit
YPBA	Young Person's Bridging Allowance

11 Index